James Balfour

Philosophical essays

James Balfour

Philosophical essays

ISBN/EAN: 9783742801166

Manufactured in Europe, USA, Canada, Australia, Japa

Cover: Foto ©Klaus-Uwe Gerhardt /pixelio.de

Manufactured and distributed by brebook publishing software (www.brebook.com)

James Balfour

Philosophical essays

OF THE

ACADEMICAL PHILOSOPHY.

THE human mind is of a nature superior to any thing that falls under our immediate observation. Its essence indeed is too subtile for our comprehension; but it is distinguished by noble powers and faculties, which exert themselves in such a manner, as to render their influence and importance abundantly conspicuous. Of these faculties the understanding appears to take the lead, as it is this intellectual principle which acquaints us with the truth of things, upon which the proper exertion of the will and active power must entirely depend. The discovery of truth

truth is naturally pleaſing and agreeable to the mind of man. But of all truths, thoſe muſt appear to be of the greateſt importance, which ſhew us the direct road to the happineſs and perfection of our nature; we have therefore the ſtrongeſt intereſt to be cautious in our inquiries after truth, as an error or miſtake may be attended with dangerous conſequences.

TRUTH is the proper object of the underſtanding: It is this faculty which inveſtigates and immediately diſcovers and perceives it; the right performance of theſe offices muſt therefore depend upon the ſoundneſs and ſtrength of the intellectual faculty. At the ſame time, we know from reaſon, as well as from the moſt undoubted experience, that the heart and affections are by no means neutral in our inquiries after truth.

PHILOSOPHY.

truth. A particular paſſion, or any affecting view of private intereſt puts the mind out of a due poſition, and creates a bias in the underſtanding. In this caſe, that fairneſs and candour which ſhould always attend an inquirer after truth, utterly forſake us, and we exert ourſelves not to diſcover impartially what is the truth, but what we wiſh and deſire ſhould be true.

Indeed, from the natural weakneſs of the human underſtanding, many truths are intirely concealed from us, and many are ſeen but very obſcurely and imperfectly; and the different degrees of this faculty in different perſons, may, in many inſtances, prove an occaſion of a diverſity in opinions.

But if we take an impartial view of what paſſes in the world, it will appear, that,

that, for the moſt part, it is the heart which is the ultimate ſource of error, and of all that variety and contrariety of opinions which prevail amongſt mankind.

PRIDE, vanity, ſingularity, a paſſionate attachment to a particular object, warp the underſtanding, and corrupt the judgement, whereby the mind is diverted from the plain paths of truth, and engaged in a fruitleſs purſuit of ſome vain phantom of imagination.

STRONG prejudices have indeed ſuch a powerful influence upon the mind, as often to determine it, even from ſlender and remote analogies, or an imperfect collection of facts, and ſome of theſe often ambiguous, to eſtabliſh a general and peremptory concluſion. And if reaſonings of this ſort are embelliſhed by an
elegant

PHILOSOPHY.

elegant and agreeable composition, and conveyed in an artful and insinuating manner, it is easy to foresee what effect they must have on those especially whose inclination or turn of thinking may give them a ready reception, and allow a small degree of probability to pass for a full demonstration.

HENCE, we may observe, that in all the different ages of the world, great parts have been no security against error; nor indeed can they be so, unless they are attended with modesty, and a sincere love of truth.

As the perception of truth, however obtained, is naturally agreeable to the mind; so, if we shall imagine, that, by the due exercise of our rational faculties, we have happily discovered any material truth, this produces an additional pleasure fure of a different kind. The circumstance of our being the discoverers, flatters our vanity; we pay a high compliment to our own understanding, and expect that others will join in it. Hence, we are disposed, not to re-examine impartially the reasons of our opinion, but to exert all our skill to defend it at any rate, as an acquisition of our own, which we are very unwilling to part with. To this, we may reasonably ascribe that tenacious adherence to many false systems and hypotheses which hath so often been observed in the present, as well as in any former ages of the world.

For the same causes will produce the same effects; and if the vanity and presumption of mankind is as great now as formerly, it will have an equal influence upon their hearts, and determine them

them to employ all their talents to maintain, with the same obstinacy, their peculiar and favourite opinions. Thus, whilst men of genius and parts, treat with scorn and contempt the prejudices and involuntary mistakes of the vulgar, which may often be more easily removed, they are, at the same time, insensible of that secret principle within their own breasts, which arms their will against the truth, and binds them fast perhaps to more dangerous errors.

As it is not necessary for our present purpose to enter into a particular consideration of the various sources of error, we shall only observe, at present, that men, either ashamed to own their ignorance, which would too much mortify the natural pride of their hearts, or, impatient of the delay of a careful examination, are commonly disposed too hastily ly to embrace some opinion upon any part of general science, and to form some hypothesis for the solution of any phænomenon, such as shall appear most plausible. From this rash and precipitate conduct, no good effect can be expected. And accordingly we find, that there was hardly any opinion so foolish and absurd, but what was taken up by some one or other of the antient philosophers, and obstinately maintained by them and their adherents.

REASON and experience, however, readily got the better of opinions so hastily embraced; and one system or hypothesis gave way to another, which, in its turn, was supplanted by a third, as that was also by its antagonist; for it was an easier matter to detect falsehood, than to discover truth. Thus philosophy was liable to perpetual uncertainty and change, and

and no fyftem could be devifed, which could long maintain its ground, unlefs from the pure obftinacy of its abettors.

This ftate and condition of philofophy very naturally produced the following confequences: Many (reflecting upon the inconftancy and uncertainty of human opinions, and that even thofe opinions which were moft fpecious, and appeared to have a folid foundation, were fucceffively exploded and abandoned) were led into this conclufion, That there was no truth in things themfelves; but that all things were toffed up and down in a giddy dance, and loft in an endlefs confufion; and that it was vain to expect any fixed object in nature, which the mind of man could lay hold of. Thus a door was opened for univerfal and abfolute fcepticifm, which totally extinguifhed reafon, and rendered the faculties of the human mind altogether infignificant and vain.

PLATO feems to have been much affected with the unhappy fate of philofophy above defcribed, and is at particular pains to find a remedy for that dangerous fcepticifm to which it leads. For this purpofe, he lays hold of the principles of the academical philofophy, which, in his Phædo particularly, he explains in a beautiful and rational manner. The general fcope of his reafoning is to the following purpofe: That if we are not able to difcover truth, this muft be owing to one of two reafons; either that there is no truth in the nature of things, or, that the mind of man, from its particular weaknefs and difeafes, is not able to apprehend it: That, upon this laft fuppofition, all the uncertainty and

and inconftancy of the judgments and opinions of mankind is eafily accounted for; and that therefore we ought to afcribe all our errors to thofe difeafes and diforders, which are apparent in the human mind, and not to any difeafe which we fuppofe, without reafon, to be in the nature of things themfelves. He obferves, that truth is often of difficult accefs: That in order to arrive at it, we muft proceed with great caution and diffidence, and carefully examine every ftep we take; and, after all, we fhall frequently find our greateft efforts difappointed, and be obliged to fit down with the confeffion of our ignorance and weaknefs.

BUT this procedure and conduct too much oppofes the natural vanity and prefumption of the human mind. In fearch after truth, men are commonly little

little difpofed to fufpect their own faculties, and impatient of difficulty or delay, they haften too fuddenly to a conclufion.

From this method of proceeding, we need not be furprifed if we fall into errors; and yet, fo apt are we to be conceited of ourfelves, that we throw the blame off from our own underftanding, and charge nature itfelf with fome latent difeafe or diforder. To prevent this bad effect, we fhould afcend to the caufe, and there apply a proper remedy. We fhould, with due care, attend to the imperfection of our faculties, and keep a ftrong guard againft the weaknefs of our hearts. We fhould examine every truth with modeft diffidence and cool deliberation, and admit nothing as fuch, but upon the cleareft evidence. If we are conftant to this method, we fhall indeed make flow progrefs gress in knowledge; but then, we shall much seldomer fall into error, or have occasion to alter our opinion. Thus rash judgement, the great cause of scepticism, will be prevented; and the cause being removed, the effect must also cease.

The principles of the antient academy, explained in this manner by Plato, appear to be of the utmost importance. They tend naturally to produce that modesty and caution which, in imperfect creatures, so liable to error and mistake, are peculiarly decent. Had these principles been universally cultivated, as they ought, many disputes in religion and philosophy would have been prevented; and even those who are thought to have employed the clearest and strongest reasoning upon matters of difficult and abstruse speculations, might have

have found good reafon to have hefitated and ftopt fhort.

THOUGH Plato was very fenfible of the weaknefs of the human underftanding, and very cautious in advancing any opinion as true; yet he was at the fame time equally fenfible of the real diftinction betwixt truth and falfehood, and that this diftinction was in many inftances clearly to be perceived by the human mind. His defign is evidently, not to introduce fcepticifm, which he confiders as the greateft diforder of our nature, but to furnifh us with a proper antidote againft it.

INDEED Plato is very ready upon moft occafions to acknowledge his ignorance; but he alfo frequently difcovers his real opinion with more or lefs affurance, according to the degree of evidence which attends

attends it. With regard to the immortality of the foul, which he particularly confiders in the forementioned dialogue, he is fenfible that his reafonings only produce a degree of probability, and infinuates the great advantage of a divine revelation with regard to this doctrine, which, like a firm vehicle, would carry us through this journey of life with much greater comfort and fecurity.

PLATO acted in an intire conformity with the wife principles which he had embraced; and whilft other philofophers were perpetually difputing about the abftrufe nature of things, with regard to which they fell into the greateft blunders, and only expofed their own ignorance, he brought his philofophy nearer home, and chiefly applied to rectify the minds and reform the manners of mankind; in doing which his more abftract abstract reasonings were corrected or supported by fact and experience; and in carrying on this excellent plan, he employed only the principles of religion, which were entirely suited to the capacities of mankind, and of which the vulgar, as well as the philosophers, might feel the influence and force.

PLATO was, on this account, justly said to have brought philosophy from heaven to earth; because, instead of employing his reasonings upon those objects which are at a distance and above our reach, he brought them home to ourselves, and applied them to much better purpose, in promoting the real happiness of men.

IT may be occasionally observed, that many centuries before Plato's days, the whole spirit and substance of this excellent

PHILOSOPHY.

lent philofophy was, by the great legiflator of the Jews, comprifed in the following fhort fentence: " Secret things " belong to the Lord our God; but thofe " things that are revealed belong to us, " and to our children for ever, that we " may do all the words of this law *." A fentence truly divine, though it fhould be fuppofed not to be infpired.

THE flighteft reflection upon the prefent circumftances of human nature, muft appear fufficient to juftify the grounds and reafons of the modeft principles of Plato. They would, however, be placed in a ftronger light ftill, if we fhould enter upon any particular confideration of the objects of the human underftanding; but this would lead us into a field equally boundlefs and perplexed. A few obfer-

* Deut. chap. 29. ver. 29.

vations, however, may not be improper.

The mind of man is indeed active and interprifing, and will hardly allow any object whatever to be beyond the fphere of its intellectual faculty: At the fame time, it fees things in a very imperfect light; yet, without adverting to this circumftance, it is apt to pronounce judgment as if its ideas were clear and compleat: A very little reflection, however, muft eafily convince us of the rafhnefs of fuch procedure.

If we carry our minds to the higheft objects of our knowledge, we fhall become extremely fenfible of their natural weaknefs and imperfection. Let us only contemplate but a very few of the divine perfections: God's manner of foreknowing future contingent events, is a thing altogether

altogether impenetrable by us, in so much that, for that reason, many deny it altogether: But in so doing, as they open a door for the greatest absurdities, so they reduce the divine to the poor standard of the human understanding; and because we can only know future events from the necessary connection of cause and effect, they will not allow God to be possessed of a different, and infinitely more perfect manner of knowledge. Such reasoning certainly proceeds upon a very false principle; and this will appear more evident, by taking a view of another of the divine perfections; I mean, creative power. That God can give existence to what formerly had none, must be admitted upon the most unquestionable principles; yet the manner of such an operation is quite inconceivable to us. But as this imperfection of our understanding is no argument against such an

act

act of divine power, there is no reason why it should be considered as any against the above mentioned species of divine knowledge.

But we shall find greater difficulties still arising from some other of the divine perfections. I shall at present only mention eternity. We cannot conceive of eternity but as an interminable successive duration; and we cannot conceive of a successive duration but as consisting of parts: But eternity can never consist of parts; for each of these parts is finite, and no number of finite parts, be it ever so great, can constitute what is infinite: For there is no proportion betwixt finite and infinite; they are altogether incommensurable. In our idea, therefore, of eternity, we absurdly confound finite with infinite, and eternity appears to be an object not barely above

bove our comprehenfion, but what even feems to involve it in a contradiction. But from this fhall we infer, that there is a real contradiction in the nature of the thing? This cannot be; for fomething eternal muft be: And the proper inference is, That the object is difproportioned to our capacity, and we are not able to regard it in a true and full light. And this ought to be the rather allowed, that in no inftance whatever, where our ideas are adequate and clear, could it ever be alledged that there was a real contradiction in the nature of things.

But it is not neceffary to afcend to the infinite perfections of God, in order to be fenfible of the great weaknefs and imperfection of our underftandings.

Let us only turn our thoughts inward on ourfelves; let us confider the nature
either

either of our souls, or our bodies, and the manner of their subsistence, and we shall find these far beyond our comprehension. If we are asked, what the substance or essence of matter is? we cannot tell. If the same question is put with regard to the soul, we are equally at a loss. That the soul is, or that it has a continued and identical existence, we know with the greatest certainty, that is, by an immediate consciousness. By this we have the clearest and most intimate perception that the principle in us which thinks, is different from every idea which is the object of thought; that it still remains when the several ideas evanish in a constant succession; that it can, however, retain these ideas for some time, reflect upon them, and compare them together, and distinguish them from one another. Thus we can, at one and the same time, hear music, see a fine garden, perceive the odor

of

of flowers, and feel cold or heat; we can compare thefe different fenfations, and prefer the one to the other. The flighteft attention, therefore, muft convince us, that what compares and diftinguifhes thefe or any other different fenfations or ideas, what ftill retains the confcioufnefs of its exiftence when thefe ideas have given place to others, muft be very different from the ideas themfelves, and muft remain and ftill exift when thefe are gone.

But, though we have this intimate knowledge of the permanent exiftence of the foul; yet how it exifts either in matter or out of matter, is a thing that paffes our comprehenfion.

Let us even defcend to thefe matters where it is allowed we have the greateft certainty, and which are the fubjects

jects of mathematical demonstration, we shall still find ourselves in many cases equally non-plussed, and be made abundantly sensible of the weakness of our faculties.

The divisibility of matter *in infinitum*, and some conclusions which are evidently deduced from that doctrine, as much confound as they enlighten our understandings. Let it be told a person not conversant about such speculations, that two lines may be drawn from two points not much distant from one another, in such a manner, that the more they are produced they shall approach nearer to one another; and yet, though produced *in infinitum*, they shall never meet *: This will be regarded by such person as a downright absurdity; yet

* Hyperbola and its asymptotes.

the

the thing is true; and though the comprehenſion of it is difficult, yet our minds are more reconciled to the truth of it, as we attentively conſider the principles upon which it proceeds.

THESE reflections might be purſued to a great length; but at preſent, I ſhall only conſider the effect they ought to have upon our minds.

WHEN by theſe we are made ſenſible how many things are removed far beyond the reach of our comprehenſion, and that, in this caſe, we are very apt to form wrong opinions, often the very reverſe of the truth; a due ſenſe of this ought to inſpire us with that habitual modeſty and caution which ſhould prevent any poſitive opinion concerning matters that are but very imperfectly apprehended by us. Philoſophers and divines, who

who form peremptory opinions in those matters of religion which are evidently abstruse and far beyond our reach, often transgress against this well established rule. Their reasonings indeed will appear sometimes very specious; but, if we ascend to their principles, we will often find them only hypothetical, or at least so imperfectly apprehended as that they cannot lay a solid foundation for a just and firm conclusion.

It is even certain, that many things we do, and must believe upon principles distinct from reason, which, if that faculty was to be consulted, it might readily oppose. Let us take an example out of a great number: The union of the soul and body we believe from an immediate perception and consciousness of it. If we were, however, to make this truth an abstract object of reason, that faculty not being

being able to difcover the nature and manner of fuch union, might be ready (however rafhly) to pronounce it impoffible and abfurd. The fame obfervation might be eafily applied to many other important truths which may ftagger our feeble reafon, yet force the affent of the mind, take hold of the heart, and influence the conduct.

We fhall further juft obferve, that, even in natural philofophy, men are unwilling to acquiefce in the poffeffion of thofe truths which their fenfes and experience have fufficiently difcovered; they would fain afcend to the fecret caufes of things; nay, they vainly imagine thefe to be qualities of natural bodies themfelves, which, however, are but mere inftruments, and totally diftinguifhed from that active principle which fets them in motion.]

But

But it appears unneceffary to carry thefe reflections any further: Enough has been faid to difcover the nature, and fhow the folid foundation of the academical philofophy, which makes modefty and caution the fupport and ornament of truth. A philofophy which, by refufing too eafy an affent, fecures us againft fcepticifm; and, by doubting in matters where there is fomething obfcure or imperfectly apprehended, makes way for the firmer and more perfect reception of truth, when ever it is fupported by fufficient evidence.

This excellent philofophy, originally derived from the ever memorable Socrates, was explained and illuftrated by Plato, who, for that purpofe, frequented a grove at a little diftance from Athens, which was confecrated to the memory of Academus, an Athenian hero, from whence

whence this philofophy received the name of Academical. From Plato it was tranfmitted through a fucceffion of feveral eminent perfons, who maintained it upon its original excellent plan; at laſt, Arcefilas received the academy.

This philofopher feems to have poffeffed an uncommon degree of fubtilty and acutenefs. His confcioufnefs of this, joined to a large fhare of vanity and conceit, feems to have determined him to defert the old principles of the academy, and to fet up upon a peculiar plan of his own. Ambitious to be the head of a fect, he appears only to have attended to the novelty and fingularity of his opinions, altogether regardlefs of the confequences fo fatal to the peace of mankind.

HE

He disputed upon each side of a question, and always thought he found equal reason to reject both. From this he was led to the following conclusion, the distinguishing, and indeed the only principle of his philosophy, That there was no distinction betwixt truth and falsehood, or at least, that the human faculties could not apprehend it.

Before I make any reflections upon the consequences of this principle, or its deviation from the old academy, it may be proper shortly to observe, that being contrary to nature, and destroying at once all the principles of action, it could not long subsist; and was therefore supplanted by Carneades, the author of the new academy, who, though he also disputed subtilely upon each side of a question; yet he was obliged to allow of the distinction betwixt probable and improbable,

probable, as a neceſſary principle of action; upon which Cicero, who was a ſtickler for this ſect, juſtifies his writing a treatiſe of offices.

As in this there appears to be truth, we ſhall make no further remarks upon this philoſophy; though, if it is allowed that there may be a reaſon to affirm an opinion to be probable, it would be no difficult matter to ſhow, that in many inſtances at leaſt, there may be an equal reaſon to affirm an opinion to be certain.

We ſhall only further juſt obſerve, that it does not appear neceſſary to take any notice of Pyrrho. His notions ſeem to have been much the ſame with thoſe of Arceſilas, though he had no concern in the academy: Only, it is ſaid of him, that he affected to ſupport his principles by his practice, and pretended to make

no

no diftinction betwixt a plain road, a river, or a precipice; which, if true, would have been fo far from gaining credit to his philofophy, that it would only have demonftrated the author of it to be a madman, and rendered it neceffary to confine him to bedlam.

We fhall now return to make fome remarks upon the doctrine of Arcefilas, and to confider how far it has deviated from the wife inftitutions of Plato.

At firft view, it may appear, that the innovation of this philofopher differs from the old academy only in degree, carrying the doubt, common to both, to a greater extreme. But if we fhall examine the matter with more attention, we fhall difcover that they are two very diftinct fpecies of philofophy, and even directly oppofite posite to one another in their principal design.

It was the great intention of the first, to point out the surest way to truth; but it was the avowed purpose of the other, to block up the avenue to truth altogether. The first recommended modesty, diffidence, and caution; virtues which imply distinction and choice: The other put all things upon the same level, or rather confounded them in one universal chaos. It was the great concern of Plato to find an antidote against scepticism, which he considered as the most dangerous disease of the mind; but scepticism itself was the grand conclusion which Arcesilas constantly had in view. Plato indeed greatly contracted our sphere of knowledge; yet he left it sufficient for the highest exercise of virtue, and all the noble purposes of life.

But Arcefilas, by deftroying this fphere altogether, annihilated at once every principle of action, and introduced an indifference iffuing in defpair. His philofophy indeed involves mankind in a more melancholy gloom than Æneas experienced in his paffage to hell.

> Ibant obfcuri, fola fub nocte per umbram
> Quale per incertam lunam fub luce maligna,
> Eft iter in fylvis, ubi cœlum condidit umbra
> Jupiter, et rebus nox abftulit atra colorem.

The fceptical philofophy muft appear to be extremely unnatural, as it will not allow us to give affent to felf-evident propofitions, which it is yet not in our power to refufe: In fuch affent the mind is paffive, and it is extorted from us whether we will or not.

And it is vain to pretend, that felf-evident propofitions are difcovered to be inconfiftent, inconsistent, and must therefore destroy one another: For this could never once be alledged in cases where our ideas were clear and adequate; and if, in other instances, there was any thing of a contrary appearance, the just conclusion to be made was, that our conceptions were imperfect and improper, and not that there was any inconsistency in things themselves.

Indeed, so unnatural is this extravagant doubt of Arcesilas, that even those who are disposed to embrace it, cannot remain long under its feeble influence; but nature must recur upon them whether they will or not, and force them to think and assent like other men; nay, we have no security from this philosophy even against the most presumptuous dogmatism: For, whilst the antient academician maintains his small but valuable stock

ſtock of truth within the entrenchments of modeſty, caution, and circumſpection, he has ſomething upon which to fix and eſtabliſh his mind; whereas the wavering diſciple of Arceſilas, under the influence of no proper principle, and having ſure hold of nothing, is more eaſily carried over to the oppoſite extreme of the moſt peremptory dogmatiſm. Of this we may have occaſion afterwards to give ſome examples.

Of the modern writers who have patroniſed the ſceptical philoſophy, none perhaps has wrote with more acuteneſs than Mr Hume. He has furniſhed us with an eſſay expreſsly upon this ſubject, intitled, *Of Academical or Sceptical Philoſophy*, confounding, by this title, two ſpecies of philoſophy, eſſentially different from one another, and which, therefore,

fore, ought to be carefully diſtinguiſhed.

But we ſhall proceed to make ſome remarks upon the reaſonings and ſentiments of this very ſubtile author. We do not, however, ſo much mean to canvaſs theſe metaphyſical arguments by which he endeavours to ſubvert the foundations of all truth and ſcience, but to point out the abſurd and even pernicious conſequences of this ſpecies of philoſophy.

With regard to the firſt, however, as he begins with diſcrediting the authority of our external ſenſes, we may obſerve, That theſe were given us not ſo much to lead us directly into the internal nature and truth of things, as to intimate to us what was immediately uſeful and agreeable to our nature; and this excellent

excellent purpose they serve in a very remarkable manner.

With regard to real existence, our reasoning is chiefly founded in the necessary connection betwixt cause and effect. This connection he endeavours to break, not indeed in the essay under view, but in another place, to which he tacitly refers: And as this topic well deserves a separate consideration, we shall not enter upon it here; but only observe, that all his efforts are but vain and fruitless attempts to root up the great pillars of nature; and the engines he makes use of for this purpose have no better support than an opinion of Mr Lock's, which is either mistaken or erroneous.

He ventures further to attack the foundations even of mathematical truth; and

and is so bold upon this subject, that it will be proper to quote his own words *: " No priestly dogmas," says he, " invented on purpose to tame and sub- " due the rebellious reason of mankind, " ever shocked common sense more than " the doctrine of the infinite divisibility " of extension, with all its consequences, " as they are pompously displayed by all " geometricians and metaphysicians, with " a kind of triumph and exultation: A " real quantity, infinitely less than any " finite quantity, containing quantities " infinitely less than itself, and so on, *in* " *infinitum*: This is an edifice so bold and " prodigious, that it is too weighty for a- " ny pretended demonstration to sup- " port; because it shocks the clearest " and most natural principles of human " reason."

* Essay of the acad. or scept. Philos.

This very bold and peremptory decifion, is a proof and fpecimen of what was formerly obferved, That the tranfition from the moft determined fcepticifm to the higheft extravagance of dogmatifm, is moft natural and eafy. It is impoffible for any dogmatift to affume a higher tone, or a bolder expreffion, than our author does upon this occafion; and yet, all this is founded on a great mifapprehenfion of the fubject he is confidering; for no geometrician ever pretended to demonftrate, that matter was divifible into real or actual parts infinitely fmall. A real quantity infinitely fmall, is certainly abfurd; for any one part of matter muft undoubtedly bear fome proportion to any other part that may be fuppofed; and confequently, cannot be infinitely lefs than it. All that geometricians demonftrate is, that matter cannot be divided into parts fo fmall but that
thefe

these are further divisible; the consequence indeed is, that matter cannot be divided into actual or real parts, which are infinitely small, directly contrary to the supposition made by our author. A great mathematician expresses himself upon this subject in the following words: * " Thus, (as we observed
" elsewhere), an absurd philosophy is
" the natural product of a vitiated geo-
" metry; for though it follows from
" our notion of magnitude, that it al-
" ways consists of parts, and is divisible
" without end; yet an actual division *in*
" *infinitum* is absurd, and an infinitely
" little quantity (even in Mr Leibnitz's
" judgement) is a mere fiction. Philo-
" sophers may allow themselves to ima-
" gine likewise, infinite orders of infi-
" nitely small particles of matter, and

* M'Claurin on Sir Isaac Newton, lib. 1. cap. 4.

" suffer

"suffer themselves to be transported
"with the idea; but these illusions are
"not supported by sound geometry, nor
"agreeable to common sense."

Our author proceeds to consider the nature of time, in which he falls into an equal absurdity. He makes the supposition of an infinite number of real parts of time passing in succession. But an infinite number is a glaring absurdity; for nothing that is infinite can consist of finite parts, which can bear no proportion to it; and indeed an infinite number is a number that cannot be numbered, that is to say, no number at all.

Indeed it must be confessed, that, in attempting to form an idea of eternity, the mind is distressed with apparent contradictions. But, from this, shall we infer, that there is a contradiction in the thing

thing itfelf? The moft natural inference furely is, That fuch contradictions are intirely the effect of our improper and imperfect conceptions of an object too big for our weak faculties.

And a reflection upon this fhould lead us back to the principles of the old academy, which admonifh us to be cautious and modeft in our decifions with regard to matters intricate and fublime, where we find our ideas to be very imperfect.

But we fhall now proceed to confider the confequences of this fceptical philofophy. The great confequence muft indeed ftrike every one at firft view. It muft introduce an univerfal lethargy and infenfibility; as it deftroys all diftinction betwixt truth and falfehood, good and evil, there can remain no principle to prompt us to action, nor any object to concern ourfelves ourſelves about: For though we ſhould believe our own exiſtence, we cannot believe the exiſtence of any thing elſe. Thus each individual would be abandoned to a ſtate of total indolence and deſpair, and the whole race of men would ſpeedily be extinguiſhed.

Our author is himſelf ſhocked with this frightful view of things, and flies with abhorrence from that miſerable philoſophy which produces it. But let us conſider what expedient he falls upon to relieve himſelf. In place of this abſolute ſcepticiſm, he ſubſtitutes what he calls a more mitigated ſcepticiſm, and which he conſiders as partly the reſult of the former, and as tending to inſpire us with modeſty, caution, and reſerve.

But this is a palpable peace of ſophiſtry; for modeſty and caution imply a diftinction betwixt truth and falfehood, though not always eafy to be difcovered; but as abfolute fcepticifm totally deftroys fuch diftinction, what place can there be for thefe virtues, or, upon what objects can they be exercifed?

Our author, in reality leads us back imperceptibly to the old academy, whofe principles indeed infpire us with modefty, and are at the fame time peculiarly calculated to guard us againft Pyrrhonifm, as has been formerly obferved.

But our author proceeds ftill to mention another fpecies of mitigated fcepticifm, and which he alfo confiders as the refult of Pyrrhonifm, by which he diftinguifhes the objects of our knowledge. But it muft be evident, at firft view, that fuch effect can never flow from a principle which

46 OF THE ACADEMICAL

which at once deftroys all truth, and confounds every diftinction whatever.

He allows, that nothing but the ftrong power of natural inftinct can free us from the force of the Pyrrhonian doubt: Now, inftinct is not a rational principle; and therefore reafon never can overcome fuch doubt. It is vain, therefore, for a Pyrrhonift to talk of a correct judgement, as our author does; for Pyrrhonifm excludes the judgement altogether, as it allows of no principles upon which it can proceed.

Nay, as Pyrrhonifm reprefents the intellectual faculty as totally unfound and difordered; it is therefore to be rejected altogether, not only in the admiffion of principles, but in every operation regarding them. It is impoffible, therefore, to extricate ourfelves from the embaraffment

baraffment and diftrefs which our author is fo fenfible we are thrown into by abfolute fcepticifm, but by returning to the deferted principles of the old academy.

Agreeably to thefe principles, we may afcribe to the human mind the faculty of intelligence, or the power of difcerning truth, as eftablifhed upon a folid foundation, at leaft in fome inftances.

It is, and always will be perceived as true, That two and three are equal to five. It is, and always will appear a certain demonftration, if duly attended to, That the three angles of a triangle are equal to two right ones. The mind may acquire the poffeffion of many truths attended with an equal evidence. But in our too eager purfuit of knowledge, we are

apt

apt to run a great rifk, either by haftily
aflenting to propofitions not duly examined,
or by ftretching beyond our
fphere in queft of objects too remote or
fublime for our narrow faculties. The
old academy warns us of this danger,
and prefcribes proper rules to guard us
againft it. It admonifhes us to keep a
firm guard againft rafh and hafty affent;
and alfo carefully to examine the ftrength,
or perhaps rather the weaknefs of our
intellectual faculties, and the proportion
they bear to the feveral objects which
may be prefented to them. We may
therefore confider the different objects
of our knowledge, in relation to this
philofophy of Plato, but not that of Arcefilas,
which excludes all difference and
diftinction whatever. We fhall accordingly
make fome obfervations upon our
author's opinion with regard to this matter.

His

His principal design indeed appears to be, to banish religion altogether from our thoughts. Its best and most solid foundation he affirms to be faith and divine revelation: And how insufficient, in his opinion, this foundation is, he has very explicitely informed us elsewhere*. He maintains, That the non-existence of any being, without exception, is as clear and distinct an idea as its existence: That it is vain to inquire into the origin of worlds: That we should leave all distant and high inquiries to the arts of priests and politicians; and that we should confine ourselves to common life, and to such subjects as fall under daily practice and experience.

But let us examine this matter upon the principles of the old academy. These

---

* Essay 10. of miracles.

principles, indeed, chiefly recommend to us an attention to common life and practice. But to what purpose do we give this attention? It muſt ſurely be in order to regulate our lives in ſuch a manner, as to procure the greateſt good to ourſelves and others; that is, to live virtuouſly. Now, the cauſe of virtue and religion are ſo intimately connected, that they cannot be ſeparated: For a juſt ſenſe of religion eſtabliſhed in the mind, is at once the ſureſt guard againſt vice, and the nobleſt motive* to virtue. It beſtows dignity and importance equally upon the objects and exertions of human conduct, and renders duty no leſs pleaſing than neceſſary: So that, without it, all the tranſactions and atchievements of mankind, and even life itſelf, have little or no value. And we muſt agree in opinion with that illuſtrious philoſopher, the Emperor Antoninus, when he aſſerts, That without

without God and Providence, life is not worth the living.

And further, thofe principles of religion which immediately influence virtue are plain and obvious to the meaneft capacities, and as fenfibly felt by the vulgar as by the moft profound philofopher. The natural movements of the heart carry us towards them, and the principle of confcience, with very little reafoning, binds them upon us in the ftrongeft manner. Every thing without us and within us, leads to the acknowledgement of a God; nor is it poffible to form a clear and diftinct idea of the non-exiftence of a firft caufe of all things, a neceffary and eternal Being.

So far was Plato, the firft publifher of the academical philofophy, from thinking, that religion had little connection with

with common life, that his fentiments were the very reverfe; and he confidered atheifm and impiety as having the moft pernicious influence upon human conduct; in fo much that, in his tenth book of laws, after diftinguifhing feveral fpecies of atheifm and impiety, he propofes that a law fhould be made, that thofe perfons who have been led to atheifm, not from the wickednefs of their lives, but fome certain fpecies of madnefs, fhould be confined to a houfe of correction for the fpace of five years; and, in the mean time, proper care fhould be taken to recover them to a juft way of thinking; but that, if after this they fhould ever be found guilty of impiety, they fhould be punifhed with death; and that thofe who to their atheifm joined a wicked and flagitious life, fhould be fhut up for life in a difmal prifon, and no free perfon fhould ever have accefs to them;

them; and that, after death, their bodies ſhould be expoſed, unburied, without the Attic territory.

ALL our author's vain though ſubtile reaſonings in relation to cauſe and effect, certainly never entered into the head of any man, ſo as to form the leaſt oppoſition to the ſtrength of that argument for the exiſtence of a Supreme Being, which naturally ariſes from the connection of cauſe and effect.

IT is this argument which alone proves the exiſtence of every thing beſides ourſelves, and which proves the exiſtence of God with more certainty than that of any thing elſe; ſo that, before we reject the opinion of a Deity, we muſt deny the exiſtence of every being but ourſelves: When therefore we diſtinguiſh the objects of our knowledge, we muſt
not

not exclude religion altogether, but ought to confider it carefully in its different lights.

Some parts of religion are so obvious and plain, and have such an essential influence upon the just conduct of life, that we will find it both our wisdom and interest to embrace and cultivate them. But there are indeed other matters in religion which rise far above our scanty faculties. In vain do we pretend to trace the amazing perfections of an infinite Being, or to determine the nature and manner of his existence. It is arrogance and presumption to censure any part of his universal administration, when our ideas of it are so very obscure and imperfect. We have often reason to suspect, that in matters of such high speculation, the truth itself is very different from those specious appearances which would
obtrude

obtrude themselves upon us as such, and to which we are apt to give too easy a reception.

Here then is the field where we cannot too much exercise the virtues of modesty, caution, and reserve; and here we find the proper use of the wise principles of the old academy, to which we cannot pay too great regard. But what an inconsistent and preposterous thing is human nature? For it is to be observed, that the sceptics themselves are often the most positive and decisive with regard to matters of the most subtile and difficult speculation; they would reduce them to the standard of their own very imperfect ideas, and from such improper premises, hesitate not to infer the conclusion. This indeed they may do often speciously, whilst men are unwilling to attend to the weakness of their faculties and

and imperfection of their ideas, and are confequently led to give too hafty an affent. But it is here where true philofophy chiefly recommends modefty and doubt; and had its precepts been duly liftened to, and properly cultivated, they would have fhut the firmeft door againft fcepticifm, and alfo prevented many ufelefs, if not hurtful, difputes among philofophers and divines.

From the obfervations already made upon the academical and fceptical philofophy, thefe two fpecies muft appear not only different from, but even contrary to one another. The firft lets fall a gentle light upon thefe truths which are of the greateft importance: The laft wraps up all things in total darknefs. The one, infpiring us with modefty and caution, preferves us from error: The other, deftroying all diftinctions, leaves the mind without

without any guard at all. The principles of the one are calculated to prevent rash assent, and positive opinion; but the other, having no foundation to fix upon, cannot secure us against even the highest dogmatism. But their difference is perhaps still more conspicuous in their effects upon the heart, than those upon the mind.

Scepticism exhausts the native strength of the soul, by withdrawing every thing that can cherish and support it: But the more auspicious academy, by placing us under the guard of providence, inspires the heart with vigour, alacrity, and hope. The one leaves us weak and defenceless in a forlorn world: But the other acquaints us, That we act under the eye and protection of an universal Parent.

WITH regard to conduct, fcepticifm confeffedly cuts all the finews of action, removes every connection with, or concern for others, and reduces us to a ftate of ftupid indifference and fullen defpair. But the better academy makes way for the exertion of all the active powers, under the influence of virtue. Indeed, with regard to the intricate nature of things, it is modeft and cautious, both in its fpeculations and decifions. But, at the fame time, it cultivates thofe affections which connect us with thofe of our own fpecies, whilft we are engaged to confider all as united under the divine adminiftration, and that not merely from abftract reafonings, but from the perception of that univerfal and admirable order which ftrikes every fenfe, and is felt by every faculty.

Can we hesitate, therefore, in our choice betwixt two such opposite species of philosophy? Reason and nature will not permit this.

Some truths are so plain and evident, that reason must assent to them; and self-love is so essential to the mind, that it will engage us in some course of action or other in pursuit of happiness.

Let us then comply with the modest philosophy of the old academy. This indeed will check the presumption of those men, who, from a conceit of their own genius, boldly decide in matters above their sphere, and thereby often lose truths which might be within their reach: But it will, however, furnish us with proper principles of action to discharge the duties we owe to God and man; in doing which we shall find ourselves animated by

by the agreeable perfuafion of that conſtant and univerſal providence of the Deity, which, (to uſe the words of an ingenious and elegant writer), * " gives
" ſtrength to our hopes, and firmneſs to
" our reſolutions, ſubdues the infolence
" of proſperity, and draws out the ſting
" of affliction: In a word, it is like the
" golden branch to which Virgil's hero
" was directed, and affords the only ſe-
" cure paſſport through the regions of
" darkneſs and ſorrow."

WE ſhall conclude juſt with obſerving, that the diſciples of Socrates made uſe of the principles of this excellent philoſophy, not only to govern and direct them in their inquiries after truth, but alſo to limit and confine theſe inquiries to the moſt important objects of it. They obſerved the large field of ſcience to be too

* Fitzoſborne's letters, letter 8.

extenſive

extensive for the weak and limited faculties of man; this reflection naturally led them to give their chief application to what most immediately tended to the perfection and happiness of their nature; and this was undoubtedly the science of morals; a science whose province it was to rectify the heart and regulate the conduct, whilst other sciences were directed to objects of a more external nature.

These philosophers, therefore, though they paid a proper regard to such sciences as were useful or ornamental in life; yet, whenever they observed these separated from virtue, (which was often the case), they accounted them fallacious and vain *, and exerted all their industry, not only to trace out the true path of virtue, but also to discover the most effectual motives to inspire the mind

* Ceb. Tab.

with conftancy and refolution proportioned to its moft arduous atchievements. And indeed, they could derive motives of this importance from no other fource than that of religion, which alone opens up truths the moft interefting and the moft univerfally felt by mankind.

THE doctrine of the immortality of the foul, in particular, they applied to this noble purpofe; whilft, after the example of their great mafter, they taught mankind, that it was vain to hope for happinefs hereafter, without ftudying at prefent to make all poffible improvement in wifdom and virtue.

OF

ACTIVE POWER.

THE intimate nature of the foul is unknown to us; neither can we comprehend how or in what manner it thinks. That it thinks, however, we have the greateſt certainty; that is, an intimate conſciouſneſs.

ALL the ideas which we naturally refer to things without us, appear to be derived from ſome kind of ſenſation or other, in the reception of which the mind is intirely paſſive. But, previous to the admiſſion of ſuch ideas, the mind appears to be poſſeſſed of ſome kind of conſciouſneſs, at leaſt of that of its own exiſtence,

existence, without which we cannot comprehend how it could be at all sensible of the impression of any thing external.

Mr Locke derives all our ideas from sensation, or from reflection upon the operations of the mind in relation to them. It may indeed be allowed, that the first notions of things are given to the mind by means of some sensation or other: But then it may also be true, that after such notices are given, the mind, by the exertion of some inherent power, may be able to discover some remarkable qualities of such things, and even things of a very different nature, which are not to be discovered merely by any sense whatever.

In the reception of our original ideas, the mind, as has already been observed,

OF ACTIVE POWER.

is intirely paffive; but, in the reception of thofe fubfequent ones, it is manifeftly active. In order to prove the truth of what we have advanced, it is not neceffary to enter into a general examination of Mr Locke's doctrine; it will be fufficient to make trial of it in a particular inftance, which fhall be that of active power, a quality of the greateft and moft univerfal importance, upon which all the changes in nature abfolutely depend.

MR LOCKE endeavours, agreeably to the principles he hath laid down, to trace the origin of our idea of active power up partly to fome fenfation, partly to fome reflection of the mind on its own operations. The fum of his reafoning is, That the mind, obferving the frequent changes made upon things, confiders in one thing the poffibility of having any of its fimple ideas changed; and in another, the poffibility

fibility of making that change; and fo comes by that idea which we call *power*.

BUT let us confider this matter with accuracy and attention. If we fuppofe that matter has in itfelf a power to begin motion, and to act upon another part of matter; yet, this power is not the object of any fenfation: All that our fenfes take notice of, is the mere motion of matter; but whether this motion is produced by matter itfelf, or fome other caufe, is what the underftanding, not the fenfes, is the proper judge of. If we fee a ftone moving in the air, fenfe indeed perceives the motion, but cannot determine whether this motion was begun by the ftone itfelf, or by fomething elfe very different from it. Our idea of power is therefore an intellectual idea, and not perceiveable by any fenfe whatever.

BUT

OF ACTIVE POWER. 67

But let us next confider reflection as the fource of our idea of power. If we fuppofe indeed, that the mind has in itfelf a power to act, and which it exerts upon proper occafions, it muft acquire the cleareft idea of power by the immediate confcioufnefs of its own operations: But, as fome pretend to queftion fuch a power of the mind, in order to avoid any difpute upon this occafion, we fhall proceed to try how the mind may otherways acquire an idea of active power.

When we obferve a change made upon any thing, it is natural for us to confider how this change has happened. In doing this, we immediately perceive, that the change muft be effected either by the thing changed itfelf, or by fome thing elfe which may be connected with it: For, if we fuppofe the thing itfelf to continue

continue as it was, and likeways exclude the influence of every other being, we clearly perceive there can be no change at all. Whilſt the ground and reaſon of its exiſtence continues the ſame, the thing itſelf muſt remain in the ſame ſtate, without any change whatever. There appears to be no propoſition that carries along with it a ſtronger degree of evidence; and any reaſoning we beſtow upon it is no more than placing it in different points of light, in which it ſtill appears with an undiminiſhed luſtre.

But as abſtract propoſitions may be apt to fatigue the mind, if we ſhall try this matter by fact and experience, it will ſtill receive the greateſt confirmation. Let us only conſider the motions of the members of our bodies: Some of thoſe are conſtantly obedient to the inclination

OF ACTIVE POWER.

clination of the will. When we will to move our finger, for example, it immediately moves in what manner we pleafe; we therefore juftly infer, that there is a real and neceffary connection betwixt the will and fuch motion of the finger. It may be obferved, that it is needlefs here to determine whether the mind is the proper caufe of this motion, or fome fuperior being effectually co-operating with it; for that does not in the leaft affect the argument. Mr Hume alledges, that in the cafe mentioned, and in all other fimilar cafes, there is only a conftant conjunction of things without any real connection; which conjunction muft therefore be purely cafual: That is, when I will to move my finger, the motion that follows has no real connection with my will, but happens only by accident, juft at the time I willed the motion; and confequently would

would have taken place whether I had willed it or not. But this is quite inconfiftent with that immediate confcioufnefs I have of the motion always taking place, and always varying according to every the leaft variation of my will; a thing altogether incompatible with mere chance. Two things indeed, that have no real connection, may exift together cafually at the fame time; but when one thing conftantly attends another, when all its variations perfectly correfpond to the meaning and intention of that other; when it ceafes to be, when that ceafes; this is the ftrongeft proof imaginable of defign and of real connection, whether mediate or immediate, and is quite beyond all the power of chance.

Thus, from a conftant obfervation of the order and connection of things, as well

OF ACTIVE POWER. 71

well as from the cleareſt intuitive perception, we acquire the idea of active power; that is, of a quality in ſome being, whereby it is able to produce a change in relation to another, and to give exiſtence to ſome new mode or thing which did not exiſt before. What produces the change we call *cauſe*, the production itſelf we call *effect*; and we conſider power as the neceſſary quality which connects theſe.

THERE are indeed no ideas more univerſally acknowledged than thoſe of cauſe and active power; even the loweſt of the vulgar, upon the appearance of any new object, is ready to put the queſtion, not if it had a cauſe, but what the cauſe of it is. And the antient philoſophers, who ſeldom agreed in any thing; yet all agreed in this, that every effect muſt have a cauſe, as Cicero, in his book *de fato*, informs us,

including

including even Epicurus himself. And indeed, the idea of active power is the only means whereby we can with certainty come to the knowledge of the exiftence of any being befides ourfelves.

Our idea of active power, as has been already hinted, is not the effect of any fenfible impreffion of external objects, in which the mind is intirely paffive; but is acquired by the action of the mind in the exercife of its intelligent faculty, whereby it difcovers, by a neceffary inference, or rather intuitive perception, that fuch a quality muft be; and in this manner alfo it difcovers many other intellectual ideas. Mr Locke's opinion as to the origin of thefe ideas, however refpectable, is not decifive: For thefe are matters to be determined by reafon, and not authority. Mr Locke admits the idea of power as unqueftionable;

OF ACTIVE POWER.

ftionable; but if it is to be derived from reflection, this word is to be taken in a larger fenfe than in what that judicious writer feems to underftand it.

OUR idea of power, however certain and real, is yet imperfect; as we cannot juftly conceive how an active being begins to exert this quality. But this is no reafon for denying the quality altogether, any more than it would be to deny that we think, becaufe we cannot explain how and in what manner we think.

BUT, as Mr Hume and fome other ingenious writers have taken an opportunity, from the imperfection of our idea of power, to take away that quality altogether, or grofsly to mifreprefent it; the fubject is of that importance as to merit fome farther examination.

THE highest degree of power is that which can give being to what before had no existence. That some things now exist which once did not exist, must be admitted, and seems to be so indeed by Mr Hume himself: But, upon pretence, that we can have no idea of power, he would lead us to believe that such things may have started up out of nothing without any cause whatever. But this reasoning contradicts and destroys itself; for most certain it is, that we can have no idea of any thing beginning to exist from nothing, without a cause; and therefore, if there is no cause, such thing, according to his reasoning, cannot exist. If, then, what is allowed to begin to exist, can neither exist with nor without a cause; it must necessarily follow, that what begins to exist does not exist at all. But if we will reason justly, we will never be involved

OF ACTIVE POWER.

volved in such a glaring contradiction. We have indeed no proper idea of a creative power; but neither can we limit the perfections of an almighty Being, or bring them down to the standard of our very weak faculties. For aught we know, such a Being may have a creative power; whereas, on the other hand, it must appear certain, that no being whatever could, of itself, begin to exist from nothing. Our clear perception of this truth is not liable to any objection arising from the imperfection of our faculties; for, let them be ever so imperfect, they can clearly comprehend, that nothing has no qualities at all; and consequently, that it can have no qualities superior to our conceptions, or that can be considered as the reason or ground of any change whatever: And thus we may clearly avoid the above-mentioned contradiction, by allowing a creative power; a thing which, though

though we cannot conceive, yet we have no reason to deny.

But we shall proceed to the consideration of another topic, which will not only throw light upon the present argument, if it needed any, but will also discover another material quality essential to any efficient cause, and that is intelligence.

Power alone is not sufficient for the production of any thing; for we cannot conceive how a being possessed of power, can exert this quality without an intention and design so to do; and intention and design evidently imply thought and intelligence. This general argument we may have occasion to resume afterwards; and therefore at present we shall confine our reasoning to a regular production.

The

OF ACTIVE POWER.

The system of this universe discovers the most amazing order and regularity in its whole contrivance; and it also every day produces new forms in which a like order and beauty is constantly observed. This could never be the effect of mere power: It necessarily implies also intelligence and design; for no degree of power whatever, acting in a blind and casual manner, could produce any regular effect at all; much less that amazing order and proportion which are every where so conspicuous through this immense universe. Intelligence therefore is as necessary as power to the production of such an effect; and it would be equally impossible to account for it if we should exclude either of these qualities.

And this is an additional proof (if such was necessary) of the necessity of a cause,

cause, in order to the production at least of a regular effect. Such a production requires intelligence as well as power. These qualities must be essentially united and jointly concur in demonstrating the necessity of a cause. Upon this occasion, it is natural to remark the superlative absurdity of Mr Hume's opinion, in supposing an effect, at least a regular effect, to begin to exist without any cause at all: For, in the first place, this opinion supposes, that all the parts of the universe took their regular station which they now occupy in a fortuitous and casual manner, which is much the same with Epicurus's fortuitous concourse of atoms; a ridiculous fiction now universally exploded.

But, further, it conjoins with this a notion still more absurd, if possible, that every thing began to exist from nothing,

OF ACTIVE POWER.

thing, without any cause at all; a strain of extravagance which never could enter into Epicurus's thoughts: For he allowed some cause (though a very improper one) of the origin of this mundane system.

Having now demonstrated, that power is a real quality which connects cause and effect; and that consequently every effect must have a cause, we shall make one general observation more upon another very extraordinary opinion of Mr Hume. That subtile writer, where he is pleased to make the supposition of cause and effect, observes, " That as the
" universe shows wisdom and goodness,
" we infer wisdom and goodness; as it
" shows a particular degree of these per-
" fections, we infer a particular degree
" of them precisely adapted to the ef-
" fect we examine; but further attri-
" butes,

"butes, or further degrees of the same "attributes, we can never be authorised "to infer or suppose, by any rules of "just reasoning."

Now, with regard to the first cause, we certainly infer other attributes than the effects themselves can show; attributes of which the effects cannot bear the least resemblance; such as eternity, necessary existence, immutability, independency, &c. If we therefore can infer these incommunicable attributes, then, by conjoining them with the former attributes, we are led to form much higher ideas of these than the effects themselves would immediately lead us to, unless we should suppose the present universe, viewed in its full extent and duration, to be the most perfect work of an infinite Being.

AFTER

OF ACTIVE POWER.

AFTER what has been said in general with regard to that remarkable quality which we call *power*, it may be of great importance to consider a little two very extraordinary exertions of it in relation to the first Cause, that is Creation, and Preservation of the world.

CREATION.

OUR senses give us the first notices of the material world, and of many of the great constituent parts of it; and a very little reflection convinces us of the constancy, order, and regularity which it every where maintains. But the mind of man, ever active and inquisitive, is not satisfied with the bare contemplation of these objects with which it is immediately affected: It pushes its researches a great deal farther, and has a natural curiosity

curiosity to know from what source and origin all things proceeded, and for what end and purpose they were made.

The supposition of the eternity of the world, is liable to so many insuperable objections, and consequently embraced by so few, that we shall not here bestow any reasoning upon it. The general, as well as the true opinion, is, that the present system of things had a beginning. Philosophers therefore have employed all their industry and acuteness, to explain how this wonderful frame of things was at first established; but all their attempts have met with such bad success, that their several opinions do not merit any particular refutation.

WITH

With regard to the antient philosophers, if any one has a mind to know their several opinions in relation to the origin of the world, he may find them in the introduction to the Universal History; and, if his patience can allow him to read them, he will meet with the grossest absurdities that could ever enter into the human mind. Instead of discovering any philosophic truth, he may indeed feel a good moral effect, and, from a deep sense of the weakness and disorder of the human faculties, may learn that modesty and caution so much recommended by the antient academy.

Neither have the modern philosophers succeeded better than the antients, notwithstanding their superior advantages.

Monsieur

MONSIEUR de CARTES amufed the world for fome time with a philofophical fcheme, which he endeavoured to render as plaufible as poffible. But, notwithftanding the additions and amendments made to it by fome who fucceeded him, that fcheme has appeared to be intirely delufive and deftitute of the leaft foundation in truth. That celebrated philofopher was never able to inveftigate that power which was neceffary to produce his imaginary virtues; nor from thefe, however complicated, was he ever able to deduce that great order of things which is univerfally eftablifhed. The great error of philofophers upon this point has been, that they have fought the principles of matter in matter itfelf, and have thereby totally confounded the caufe with the effect.

OF ACTIVE POWER.

It is the proper province of a natural philosopher, to discover the real order of things, to examine the constant course of Nature, and to investigate those laws by which she is so invariably governed. In doing this, experience and observation must be of the greatest use, and will either prevent or correct the errors into which fancy and imagination is so apt to betray us.

The slightest reflection will convince us, that neither matter nor the human mind could be eternal. The mutable, dependent, and arbitrary condition of these are absolutely incompatible with the nature of an eternal Being. Their existence must therefore have had a beginning; and the transition from nothing to real existence must have been instantaneous, as there can be no medium betwixt existence and non-existence.

It

It muſt therefore give us the higheſt idea of the power of the firſt Cauſe, whoſe almighty command could inſtantaneouſly give being to what before had no exiſtence; though it muſt be acknowledged, that this idea is very imperfect, and inadequate.

It was arbitrary in the firſt Cauſe of all, either to have inſtantaneouſly produced the material world in its perfect form, or otherways to have brought it to that form by ſome gradual operation. That the laſt was the caſe, is the opinion univerſally received. It has always been thought, that from a chaos, or confuſed jumble of the different parts of matter, this world was, by ſome gradual procefs, brought at laſt into that ſtate of order and beauty in which it now appears. But in explaining this procefs, philoſophers, even thoſe who admitted of a

firſt

OF ACTIVE POWER.

first Cause, have always thought it necessary to call in the aid of what they term natural causes; that is, certain powers or qualities of matter, which they suppose to have a natural tendency to order and perfection, and whereby they imagine, that the operation of the first Cause may at least be assisted. But the supposition of such natural causes is purely chimerical and imaginary, as we shall afterwards have occasion to show: At present, however, we shall take them for granted, and consider of what use they could be in the original formation of this universe.

WITHOUT entering into any general examination of such natural powers or causes, we shall single out two of the most remarkable, and of the most universal influence. These are the centripetal and centrifugal forces.

BESIDES

88 OF ACTIVE POWER.

Besides the influence which thefe have upon the leffer parts of matter, it is acknowledged, that all the regular motions of the heavenly bodies, which produce the great order of the univerfe, abfolutely depend upon the proper combination of thefe powers. Now, if we will allow ourfelves to reflect, thefe powers could be of no ufe in the original formation of the world; but, on the contrary, would prove immediate obftacles to it. For example, if the heavenly bodies were placed at too great a diftance from the centre of gravity, the centrifugal force not having a fufficient counterpoife, would carry them off from the centre altogether. On the other hand, if they were placed too near that centre, they would rufh into it from the prevailing force of gravitation: At any rate, their motions would be in orbits fo excentric, as foon to prove fatal

OF ACTIVE POWER.

tal to every living thing they contained. And in any of thefe cafes it is evident, that the conftitution of a regular fyftem would be impracticable.

In order to obtain that great and beautiful effect, the heavenly bodies muft be placed at due diftances from their common centre; in confequence of which, the powers under confideration will properly counterbalance one another, and, from their juft compofition, produce all thofe excellent effects which we now experience. The fyftem of the world muft therefore be brought to its full perfection before there could be the leaft room for thefe natural caufes: Their action at any time prior to this, could produce nothing but confufion and diforder. This reafoning is alfo eafily applicable to any other fuppofed natural caufes. It is therefore vain and abfurd absurd to call in the aid of such causes to concur with the great first Cause, whose power is in itself all-sufficient and irresistible. And indeed, it is not to be wondered at, if this capital error, in explaining the original constitution of things, has led philosophers of all ages into so many absurd and even ridiculous opinions.

We must, however, upon this occasion, do justice to one very illustrious writer, who alone perceived and discovered to mankind the great truths which we have been considering. Moses, the great legislature of the Jews, informs us, that God, at the beginning, brought all things into being from nothing, by a single act of his sovereign will. A truth, which, though certain, seems hardly to have been discovered by any of the antient philosophers. The
same

fame divine author informs us, that after the matter of the world was produced, the almighty Creator, by a gradual procefs, brought it into that regular order and perfect form which it has ever fince maintained, and that, by a fimple act of his fovereign will, without the fmalleft intervention of thofe powers and qualities of matter, concerning which other philofophers have thrown out fo much abfurd and unintelligible jargon.

THAT GOD, if he had thought fit fo to do, could have inftantaneoufly produced the world in its compleat ftate of order and perfection, cannot be doubted. But one great reafon, why the fupreme Creator chofe rather to do it by a gradual and fucceffive operation, appears to be, that the intelligent fpirits who pre-exifted that grand event, might have

have an opportunity leisurely to contemplate and admire such an amazing exertion of divine wisdom and power. And accordingly, we are assured, that upon this great occasion, " the morning " stars sung together, and all the sons of " God shouted for joy *." This consideration also discovers the great propriety of the Mosaic representation, in which Light is taken notice of as the first of the regular works of God; for some such medium may have been fit, and even necessary, to render visible to the heavenly spectators the gradual advances of this grand work to a state of full perfection.

THE sublimity of the Mosaic account has been taken notice of by Longinus, that celebrated critic: Its philosophic

* Job chap. xxxviii. ver. 7.

OF ACTIVE POWER.

truth muft appear as confpicuous from the preceeding reafonings.

There is one circumftance in the Mofaic account, which, though not a proper fubject of abftract reafoning, feems to be of that importance as to merit our attention. He informs us, that God beftowed fix days in compleating the form of the world, and refted from this great work upon the feventh. The knowledge of this could only have been received by revelation; and that this was the belief and perfuafion of mankind concerning the origin of things, will appear evident, not only from the authority of Homer, and fome other of the ancient poets who have affirmed it; but chiefly from this confideration, that almoft all the different nations of the world have agreed in a period of time confifting of feven days, and have even agreed

agreed in the precife order of that period[*]. This is not to be accounted for but from fome common and great caufe; and is the more remarkable, that though the feveral nations differed in their calculations of months and years, which have yet a juft ftandard in the nature of things; yet they exactly agreed in the period of weeks, though not founded on any natural phænomena, but appearing entirely arbitrary. The caufe of this remarkable confent clearly appears from what Mofes informs us; nor can we conceive how it is otherways to be accounted for.

HAVING therefore made thefe few obfervations upon the power of the firft Caufe, as exerted in the Creation of the world, we fhall proceed alfo to confider

[*] Ufher's letters, l. 105.

a little the same power, as displayed in the Preservation and Government of it.

PROVIDENCE.

However necessary the power of the first Cause may be in the original production of things; yet some contend, that the system is brought to such a degree of perfection in its first constitution, as that it afterwards can make a shift for itself, and readily comply with certain supposed general laws, established for the regular direction of the natural world; nay, nothing is more common than to talk of natural causes, or certain powers and properties of matter, by means of which all the phænomena of nature are to be accounted for, without having recourse to the influence of the first Cause.

But

OF ACTIVE POWER.

But such opinions as these will, upon due consideration, appear to be the effect of a careless and superficial way of thinking, and altogether inconsistent with the real nature of things.

Our reasoning on this subject will be both more clear and concise, if, instead of pursuing a general argument, we shall have a particular instance more immediately in view. We shall then consider the nature of gravity, as being an universal property of matter the effects of which are of the greatest extent.

It is now an acknowledged determination in philosophy, that all bodies gravitate towards one another in a certain proportion, and according to an invariable law. But the question is, What is the cause of this universal property? Or what power is it which makes bodies

OF ACTIVE POWER.

bodies move in such a constant and regular manner? We need not here have recourse to a subtile æther as the cause of gravity: For, in the first place, it appears hardly possible to conceive, that such an æther could move these prodigious orbs with so great velocity, and at the same time with such unerring regularity: But then, if we could conceive this, it would be but removing the question a step further, in order to know what was the cause of the motion of this æther.

Let us then consider gravity as an original effect, and the power that produces it must either be in matter itself or without it. Let us examine the first of these suppositions, that the power which produces gravity is in matter itself. Now, matter is known to us only from experience and observation; and from all the observations

servations we are able to make, it appears to be entirely inert and paffive. When at reft, it continues fo till put in motion by fome foreign caufe; and when put in motion, it continues to move till ftopt by fome contrary force: So that natural philofophers have univerfally agreed to apply to matter the foregoing epithets of *paffive* and *inert*. And yet many of thefe philofophers have (though moft inconfiftently) on other occafions fuppofed matter to contain in itfelf certain active powers, which they confider as the natural caufes of particular fenfible effects.

It may however be faid, that, for aught we know, matter may contain in itfelf fuch active powers, though we are not able to perceive them. But, in the firft place, this is an affirmation without any reafon at all to fupport it; and therefore

OF ACTIVE POWER.

therefore ought to gain no credit. But, farther, let us confider whether fuch powers are not altogether incompatible with the known properties of matter. To begin motion, feems evidently to imply defign and intention: For we find it impoffible to conceive how any being can begin motion without meaning and intending to do fo; therefore, as matter is incapable of thought, and confequently of intention and defign, we muft, agreeably to all the ideas we can form, pronounce matter to be incapable of beginning motion. Whoever, therefore, affirms that matter itfelf begins motion, cannot give the flighteft reafon for this opinion, which he muft even acknowledge to be unaccountable.

But let us confider the properties of matter more particularly. Every part of matter evidently confifts of an indefinite

finite number of fmaller parts; before therefore any part of matter can begin motion, every part of that matter muft at one and the fame time begin to exert the moving power; for it cannot be faid that one particular part of the body is poffeffed of this moving power, whilft all the other parts are without it; for befides that fuch particular part is alfo compofed of other parts, we cannot afcribe a moving power to it, confidered merely as a material fubftance; for in this refpect every other part muft be equally fufceptible of the moving power, if fuch power flows from a merely material quality: But if it is to be derived from a different fource, then the principle of motion cannot be in matter, but in a fubject of a very different nature.

OF ACTIVE POWER.

In consequence of this reasoning, we must admit the truth of what was above observed, that before any part of matter can begin motion, every part of matter must begin at one and the same time to exert its moving power, and this it must also do in the same line of direction; otherways a contrariety of the powers, by counterbalancing one another, would prevent motion altogether, or at least nothing but the most confused and irregular motion could be expected. Now, if we reflect upon the preceeding observations, before any part of matter can of itself accomplish the most simple species of motion, viz. that in a right line, there must be a concurrence of an almost infinite number of different circumstances, and those altogether beyond the power of any particular part of matter: For, in the first place, every part of the matter to be moved must exert the moving

moving power at one and the same time. Now, as thefe parts are innumerable, and equally independent upon one another, fuch a general exertion of the moving power, in one and the fame point of time, can never be the effect of any quality in any particular part of matter: For, though we fhould fuppofe that part of matter capable to move itfelf; yet it could not be the caufe of motion in the other parts, which muft equally, and in the fame manner, be poffeffed of that principle. As, therefore, we cannot find the caufe of fuch a general effect in matter itfelf, we muft fearch for it in a very different principle: And indeed, this muft be a principle not only fimple and immaterial, but alfo defigning and intelligent: For a general effect, including the motion of innumerable particles of matter at one and the fame time, could not proceed

OF ACTIVE POWER. 103

proceed from a cause operating at random or fortuitously; but must unquestionably be the effect of intelligence and design.

This whole reasoning will receive additional force, if we add, that besides the indefinite number of parts to be moved at one and the same time, there are also an indefinite number of lines for the direction of that motion, one of which must be chosen or determined for all and every one of these parts; and this will necessarily lead us to the acknowledgement of an universal and designing cause, whose power all the innumerable parts of matter must instantaneously obey, and that in one and the same line of direction.

To this grand conclusion we are necessarily led even by the most simple species of

of motion. But it will appear ftill in a more ftrong and ftriking light, if we make but the flighteft reflection upon thofe various and admirable powers which are actually employed in eftablifhing and maintaining the great order of the univerfe. Gravity is a principle which is not only neceffary to the regular motion of the planets, but appears to affect every particle of matter, at leaft within our fyftem. This leads a great mathematician * to make the following juft obfervation:
" This one principle, (viz. gravity), fo
" regularly diffufed over the whole,
" fhows one general influence and con-
" duct, flowing from one caufe equally
" active and potent every where."

But in order to maintain the planets in their proper orbits, befides gravity, a
projectile

* M'Claurin upon Newton, lib. 3. cap. 4.

OF ACTIVE POWER.

projectile or centrifugal force is necessary; and this force must vary according to the distances of the planets from their common centre; and these distances must be determined from two considerations: First, The distances of the planets from the common centre must be suited to their nature, and the utility of their inhabitants. Secondly, They must be at such distances from one another, as to prevent any improper mutual influence which would be productive of great disorder. When the distances are thus determined, the centrifugal force must be impressed in a due proportion to those distances; it must be stronger upon those planets which are nearest the sun, and weaker upon those which are at a greater distance, and that not in the single reciprocal proportion of the distances, but in proportion to their gravities, which

are

are reciprocally as the squares of their distances. Now, all this admirable order, these wise and various laws of motion have been originally established, and constantly maintained with such exactness, as that the heavenly bodies, though moving with inconceivable velocity, have yet been retained in their proper orbits since their original creation, with the most unerring regularity. It seems hardly possible to reflect upon these things without being convinced, in the most irresistible manner, of the necessity of one Supreme, Intelligent, and Powerful Cause of all; a truth which, as has been already observed, we are necessarily led to, even from the consideration of the most simple species of motion.

CICERO, in his first book, *De Finibus*, makes the following very proper observation

servation upon the philosophy of Democritus and Epicurus: " Quanquam utriusque quum multa non probo, tum illud inprimis, quod, quum in rerum natura duo quærenda sint, unum, quæ materia sit, ex qua quæque res efficiantur; alterum, quæ vis sit, quæ quidque efficiat: De materia disseruerunt, vim et causam efficiendi reliquerunt."

These atomical philosophers have, according to this just observation of Cicero, confined their reasonings to the effects which might be produced by matter when put in motion; but did not consider, with any degree of attention, how matter was originally put in motion. Had they done this, they must have been necessarily led to the acknowledgement of a very different and much more noble principle; a principle possessed of power and intelligence, by whose influence alone

lone it was poffible for matter to be put in motion.

And indeed, this great principle which we are fearching after, can be no other than the power of the firft Caufe; for its influence is univerfal over all the matter in the mundane fyftem, as to fome effects, particularly that of gravity; and as to others alfo, it acts regularly in the fame manner when-ever the fame conftruction of parts takes place.

This univerfal principle of motion muft therefore neceffarily be under the immediate direction of that Supreme Wifdom and Intelligence which prefides over the whole, and by which the order and conftancy of the univerfe is invariably maintained.

Cicero

OF ACTIVE POWER.

Cicero reasons in a very just and elegant manner concerning this great principle which we are now considering, in the following words, in his pleading for Milo: " Est, est profecto illa vis; ne-
" que in his corporibus, neque in hac
" imbecilitate inest quiddam, quod vi-
" geat ac sentiat, et non inest in hoc
" tanto naturæ tam præclaro motu, nisi
" forte idcirco esse non putant, quia
" non apparet ac cernitur: Proinde
" quasi nostram ipsam mentem qua sa-
" pimus, qua providemus, qua hæc ipsa
" agimus ac dicimus, videre, aut plane
" qualis sit, aut ubi sit, sentire possimus."

Some, without any just reason, have formed an imaginary notion of what they call a *plastic nature*, appointed by God for the general direction of the universe. This opinion seems to have flowed from the vain conceits of the Epicureans,

reans, who thought the government of the world gave real trouble to the Deity; or perhaps the afferters of it thought, that it was not worthy of God to preferve that world which he thought reafonable to create. Indeed, as we ourfelves are confcious, that we have fome tafk affigned us in that portion of the univerfe which is allotted to us, we may reafonably allow, that other intelligent natures may have different employments, fuitable to their particular condition: But to afcribe to any finite being an univerfal power over all the works of nature, feems greatly to exceed any idea we can poffibly form of the higheft created intelligence.

But we are now prepared to confider what is the meaning of a *Natural Caufe*, an expreffion which we fo frequently meet with. Thofe who ufe this expreffion sion seem to have been at little pains to explain what they mean by it. If they had, they would probably have avoided a great deal of that error and confusion into which it has led them. By talking so much of natural causes in a vague manner, they seem to have made way for some obscure idea of certain latent qualities in matter, whereby it was able of itself to produce a variety of particular effects: But, from the doctrine above explained, this is absolutely impossible: It is altogether inconsistent with the known properties of matter, that it should be the real and efficient cause of any thing whatever; and it is paying a vain compliment to the Deity, to suppose he can transfer his prerogative of governing the world to a subject absolutely incapable of active power. Matter can only be an instrument; but the power of acting upon it, and setting

it

it in motion, muſt be ſought for in a principle quite different from matter.

A material inſtrument or machine may conſiſt of many parts, which communicate an impreſſed motion in a regular manner, till at laſt a particular effect is produced. Theſe parts are ſometimes ſaid to be the cauſes of the motion of the ſubſequent parts: But this is only a looſe manner of expreſſion; for, ſtrictly ſpeaking, they are but mere inſtruments in conveying the motion, whereby at laſt an intended effect is produced. But the proper and efficient cauſe of this effect is the power which firſt put the machine in motion, which we in vain ſearch for in the machine itſelf.

It is in this manner only, that we can account for all that variety of regular

lar effects discoverable in the natural world, such as gravity, electricity, vegetation, explosion, and many others that might be named; it is alone the energy of an universal Providence that can be the proper cause of them. Thus divine energy must be allowed to pervade and actuate all the parts of the universe, and that every moment. This universal cause indeed operates in a regular manner, and according to fixed and steady laws, that men may have an opportunity of exercising their rational faculties; and, from the knowledge of these laws acquired by experience, may trace the distant and future effects.

And this is properly the subject of natural philosophy, which examines the structure and compound parts of material objects, the laws of motion by which they are governed, and the regular effects which are thereby produced. It is evident, that our senses are the chief foundation of this science; we must pursue it by constant experiment and observation otherways we will run the greatest risk of substituting our own vain conceits in the room of solid truth. Indeed, it must be owned, that the compound parts of natural bodies are so extremely subtile, and of such a delicate contexture, that our senses, though assisted by every artificial improvement, can penetrate but a very little way into that exquisite machinery which is made instrumental in the production of every natural effect. These our senses, however, are what we must chiefly consult in explaining this amazing mechanism, which every the least particle of matter seems to be possessed of.

BUT

OF ACTIVE POWER.

But when we would trace the proper cause of such effects, we must ascend to a higher sphere, and leave our senses far behind. The principle of action, as well as that of thought, is too refined for our corporeal senses; it is to be sought for without and beyond matter, and is only an object of pure intelligence. And thus it must evidently appear, that the Divine Power is the great principle and spring of action in the universe. It must also appear, that nothing could be more absurd than the attempt of those philosophers, who had recourse to what they called *Natural Causes*, in order to exclude the agency of the first Cause. This was, in reality, to substitute mere non entities in the room of that Supreme Wisdom and Power which the nature of the thing absolutely required. We shall here exhibit only one specimen of this very absurd philosophy. Lucretius expresses

expresses himself in the following manner:

> Quis regere immensi summam, quis habere profundi
> Indu manu validas potis est moderanter habenas?
> Quis pariter cœlos omnes convertere? et omnes
> Ignibus æthereis terras suffire feraces?
> Omnibus inque locis esse omni tempore præsto?

THESE verses may perhaps please the imagination; but the effect they have on the judgement must be very different. Upon pretence that the great operations which he there mentions are superior to the power of the Deity, he excludes the Deity altogether, that he may resolve them all, agreeably to his avowed principles, into certain properties of matter, or rather into names which have no real meaning at all. Does it require a greater power than the Supreme Being is possessed of to govern the

the world, and shall we yet find such a power in mere matter itself? or rather, is such an effect so easy as to require no exertion of power at all? Thus he lands himself either in a glaring absurdity or flat contradiction.

NATURE is often talked of by such philosophers as a wonderful enchantress, that can raise up every form at pleasure: But if those who talk so, will attempt to explain what they mean by nature, they will find it a mere name without any meaning at all, unless they consider it as the constant influence of the Supreme Creator over the works of his own hands.

INDEPENDENT of this influence, what can nature do? Can the passion-flower, by a natural skill in geometry, describe its various and regular circles? Can the tulip,

tulip, of itself, make choice of the tints and arrangement of its beautiful colours? Does the cedar and the pine rife to heaven by their own strength? Or, do the seasons, so beneficial in their variety, by a particular agreement, divide the year among themselves? No; these are the works of Him " that formeth " the mountains, and createth the wind, " and declareth unto man what is his " thought; that maketh the morning " darkness, and treadeth upon the high " places of the earth." The beautiful appearances and agreeable vicissitudes of things, when accompanied with the slightest reflection, form that language which proclaims a Deity to mankind; and the sentiments of religion, which are thus naturally excited in the minds of the vulgar, are strengthened and confirmed by the most authentic sanctions of reason and philosophy.

OF ACTIVE POWER.

The firm and inconteſtible conſequence of all the above reaſonings is, that as the power of the firſt Cauſe was neceſſary in the creation of the world, the ſame power is equally neceſſary in the preſervation and government of it. This power muſt extend every moment to all the parts of the univerſe, the ſmalleſt particles of matter not excepted. A mere general providence, if duly examined, is a name without any meaning; and ſuch a notion, though embraced by many writers of no inconſiderable character, can yet only be the effect of a very careleſs and ſuperficial way of thinking. The divine influence muſt conſtantly pervade, actuate, and direct whatever exiſts. And nothing is more philoſophically true, than that " in God we live, " move, and have our being; and that " not ſo much as a hair of our head can
" fall

"fall to the ground without our hea-
"venly Father."

THIS indeed is a truth which readily offers itfelf to the natural fentiments of mankind, and is accordingly celebrated by feveral of the ancient poets. Many philofophers, affecting to be wifer than others, have indeed obfcured it by their vain reafonings, and endeavoured to transfer the divine prerogative of governing the world to certain occult qualities, and unknown properties, which muft yet be devoid both of activity and intelligence.

UPON this occafion, we may make a remark upon a very extraordinary opinion of Mr Hume's in relation to miracles. That fubtile writer allows a miracle to be a violation of the known laws and eftablifhed courfe of nature;
but

but he is pleased to insinuate, that we have no reason to affirm that this course and these laws of nature can be altered even by an almighty Being *; in which case, a miracle must be impossible. No insinuation perhaps ever was so bold as this; and at the same time so destitute of the least foundation. This indeed must appear when we reflect that nothing can be more easily conceived than a real change in the present course of things; and that since even a man has power to make a body move upwards, contrary to its natural gravity, to refuse the same power to an almighty Being, must be an infinite absurdity. But farther, if, in consequence of the preceeding reasoning, we consider, that God is the real and constant cause of all the regular motions in the universe, these must certainly

---

* Essay of miracles, note last.

certainly be intirely in his power; and may confequently be altered by him at his pleafure. Nay, a miracle may be performed without any exertion of divine power at all; a bare fufpenfion of this power in any particular inftance, muft produce a miraculous change, as a total abftraction of it would diffolve the univerfe. It is as eafy therefore for God to perform a miracle, as it is to maintain the prefent courfe of nature. And with whatever certainty the regular courfe of nature may be from conftant experience difcovered; yet, as this is not inconfiftent with the poffibility of a miracle, fo, whenever this laft may take place, it is as capable of a fatisfactory proof as the former; and as they are very confiftent though different truths, the evidence of the one cannot ftand in the leaft oppofition to that of the other.

WE

OF ACTIVE POWER.

We shall conclude this subject with some general reflections upon the importance of this remarkable quality of active power.

It is a quality which seems essential to a rational nature; and, without it, reasoning and reflection cannot possibly be conceived. We may suppose a being capable of receiving sensations and ideas from the impressions of foreign objects; but in that case, what would be the condition of such a being, if destitute of active power? It would be but a mere passive subject of such impressions, and could at best only be stupidly fixed in such sensations as these might produce. It would be no better than soft wax, which can indeed receive any figures from the application of external objects; but then it must also retain these according to their original impressions, without being

ing able to make the least change or variation in any of them. If we should suppose such a merely intelligent or rather sensitive being to look up to the heavenly bodies, how would it be affected? It could only perceive certain sensible ideas, containing in themselves nothing regular or grand. It could have no notion of the real magnitude, distances, or periodical courses of these heavenly bodies. It could not have the least suspicion of a magnificent universe established and maintained by the most perfect order. Nay, if we should suppose such a being capable to receive ever so great a number and variety of sensible ideas, and even to recollect them when lost; yet without active power, it could never examine them with attention; it could not transpose, disjoin, compound, or vary them any manner of way whatever; neither could it compare them so as to difcover their innumerable relations. Such a large ftock of ideas as is fuppofed, would be to fuch a being nothing but a deformed wafte, a confufed chaos, where nothing of order, beauty, or good, is to be perceived. But let a certain degree of active power be communicated to this fuppofed fenfitive being, what illuftrious effects muft this produce! It will now reflect upon its ideas; it will place them in every point of view; it will compare them and confider their various connections and agreements; it will be led even to examine their fource and origin.

This active operation of the mind will, with a kind of creative energy, bring order out of confufion, and prefent to our view a fair, regular, and magnificent univerfe, where before we felt only fome fenfible impreffions of little

tle importance, and without order or defign; nay, by means of this conjunction of intelligence and active power, we are formed for higher contemplation ftill: We are able to trace the remote caufes of things, and to difcover their connection with the effects: We overleap thofe limits which confine the whole brute fpecies, rife above all created objects whatever, and afcend to the firft great Caufe of all. Here we difcover the pureft fources of fentiment and affection, the nobleft motives of virtue, and the moft fublime objects of contemplation; we even venture to explore thofe divine perfections which in no degree can be communicated to any creature, and to which we can find nothing that bears the leaft refemblance in reflecting upon what paffes within our own minds. Neceffary exiftence, independency, immutability, eternity, we apply

ply to God, and to him alone. The contemplation indeed of such infinite perfections is apt to confound and overwhelm our created faculties; yet our ideas of them, however imperfect, are still so certain as that we are thereby enabled clearly to distinguish them from every thing else.

We form even some idea of eternity itself, perhaps, one of the most astonishing of the divine perfections. This idea is indeed but negative; yet it is such as clearly discovers eternity to be different from any periods of time whatever, which can bear no manner of proportion to it. Thus, with strict philosophic truth, it is said of God, that in his sight a thousand years are as one day, and one day as a thousand years; for these distinctions of time, when compared with eternity, are totally lost and annihilated.

annihilated. Therefore, in order to form the trueſt idea of eternity which the human mind is capable of, we are obliged to throw away all benefit we can receive from the idea of ſucceſſive duration, which by us is always conceived as conſiſting of parts; whereas eternity cannot conſiſt of parts at all. The idea of eternity is therefore a purely intellectual idea, riſing above all ſenſation whatever; nor can we, reflecting upon our own minds, find any thing there that bears the leaſt reſemblance to it.

From the preceeding obſervations, the importance of active power, in relation to the underſtanding, muſt be ſufficiently apparent; and particularly, that we are thereby enabled to acquire new ideas not ariſing from any ſenſation, nor even from reflection, at leaſt in the reſtricted ſenſe in which this has been conſidered

considered by Mr Locke. In the following essay we may have occasion to take some notice of its influence upon the will and affections, **whereby** it will appear to be the true source of the very important qualities of **Liberty** and **Morality**.

OF

LIBERTY and NECESSITY.

THERE is perhaps no object of our knowledge more interesting than that of the human mind itself; and it has this peculiar advantage, that we receive the notices of it not merely from general and abstract reasonings, but from an intimate and immediate consciousness. At the same time, this immaterial being is so delicate and subtile in its nature, and possessed of such extraordinary powers and qualities, that our ideas and views of it are at best but very imperfect and obscure; and therefore all our inquiries concerning it ought to be conducted with the greatest modesty and caution.

PHILOSOPHERS, in order to take a more exact furvey of the human mind, have generally diftinguifhed the principal faculties of which it is poffeffed; and thefe are commonly fuppofed to be the Underftanding and the Will. This diftinction, perhaps, may ferve fome good purpofes, as it confines the mind to more fimple views of its object, and thereby prevents too great a diftraction of thought; but if it is not accurate and exact, it may alfo prove the fource of capital errors; which, perhaps, is the cafe here: For befides the underftanding and the will, one important faculty of the human mind appears to be the power of acting, without which the two former feem to be eafily enough conceived; and the bad confequences of neglecting this laft faculty will eafily appear, if we confider the nature of the other two.

To the understanding all our original ideas are commonly referred, and in the production of these, the mind is allowed to be intirely passive. The will is considered as the seat of our inclinations, our desires, and aversions; and these are excited in us by their respective objects, independent of the will itself; in which therefore the mind is also passive. By this confined view of the faculties of the mind, liberty will be totally excluded; we must therefore admit the power of acting to what it can only be referred; a power of which we are immediately conscious, which secretly mixes itself with the other faculties, and communicates that vigour and energy to the mind, without which the understanding would be stupid and idiotical, and the desires and inclinations prove altogether fruitless and abortive.

BUT

But as the mind is in itself simple and indivisible, it does not seem to be of importance to our present subject to give any particular attention to the distinction of its faculties; we shall therefore carry on our reasoning without such view, and endeavour to examine with accuracy the famous question concerning Liberty and Necessity.

It seems to have been a question from the early ages of the world, Whether man was a free agent; that is, had in himself a proper principle of action? or if he was to be considered only as a very curious and extraordinary machine, whose movements and operations were all under the necessary influence of some foreign power? A sense of the constant dependence of man upon the Deity might have produced the last opinion, though other less honourable causes may have concurred.

The

The firſt opinion ſeems naturally to ariſe from the conſciouſneſs of our own minds when we engage in any kind of action; and as this conſciouſneſs is immediate, and always attends us, this opinion therefore ſeems to have been the moſt common and prevailing one.

This matter was of too great conſequence to be overlooked by philoſophers; and accordingly, they have made it an object of their particular examination. In conſequence of which, they embraced different opinions, whilſt the greater part were aſſerters of Liberty; but others, of no ſmall note, particularly the Stoicks, maintained the doctrine of Neceſſity.

Many very ſubtile and ingenious moderns have thought fit to patronize this laſt opinion; and as they have entered
into

AND NECESSITY.

into the argument with more accuracy and acuteness, we shall chiefly have in view their reasonings upon this subject.

INDEED, it must be confessed, that when dissatisfied with the opinion which naturally arises from the immediate consciousness of our own minds, we would trace the matter to its remote source and origin, and would explore the true and proper, though latent springs of action, these appear to be so delicate and subtile, that no sense can apprehend them; and even the understanding itself is fatigued and embarrassed in the difficult research.

As this is evidently the case, we ought surely to be modest and cautious in our decisions, and particularly upon our guard that we be not imposed upon on by a specious sophistry instead of solid reasoning. And perhaps, after all our nice and intricate speculations, we shall find that there is more reason to trust those natural sentiments which are suggested by an immediate consciousness, than the uncertain conclusions which flow from premisses so imperfectly understood.

But we shall now proceed to the examination of this important subject, though with that caution and brevity which its arduous and obscure nature demands.

In order to pursue the argument with clearness and precision, the first thing proper to be done, is to examine with due care and attention our ideas of Liberty and Necessity. As they are simple ideas, and not capable of definition, we shall best understand them if we trace them

them to their source and origin. And it will appear, that they arise from the different views under which cause and effect are presented to the mind. If we consider the effect as such, it is intirely passive, and is produced by the cause, whether it will or not; and this suggests to us the idea of necessity, which denotes a circumstance or quality of the existence of a thing, when considered as what could not but exist. But the nature of the cause is very different; as such, it is independent, it is not acted upon, but acts itself upon the effect; and therefore, in this view, we discover a quality or circumstance opposite to that necessity which is observed in the effect. And thus we acquire the proper idea of liberty in considering the beginning of action, or the first exertion of active power.

WHEN we obferve the movements of a mere machine, thefe appear to be neceffary; that is, they unavoidably take place in confequence of the action of fome proper caufe; and thus this neceffity is plainly relative to fomething different from the machine, and upon which all its movements entirely depend. But the action of the caufe is of a different nature; there is nothing prior to it, upon which it can depend; the caufe in its firft action is purely fimple and original; we cannot go a ftep beyond it to connect it with any thing prior to it, otherways fuch thing would be the caufe, and the other would be only an effect, and part of the fuppofed machine.

THUS we have the idea of neceffity from the manner of the exiftence of an effect; but the idea of liberty arifes from the original exertion of active power,
which

which is of a nature intirely oppofite to the firft.

THE idea of liberty, therefore, has a fource as certain and clear in the nature of things, as that of neceffity, and which is alfo prior to it in the order of nature. Thus, when we take a fimple view of the origin of thefe different ideas of liberty and neceffity, there appears to be as juft a foundation for the one as for the other; and alfo, that the one is placed in a direct oppofition to the other. One fhould imagine, therefore, that it was impoffible to confound thefe two ideas, or rather to fink the idea of liberty into that of neceffity. But the circumftance which has occafioned fuch endlefs difpute in this matter feems to be, that though we are intuitively certain, that there muft be a power in fome being, by the exertion of which it is enabled

abled to produce a particular effect; yet the precife manner of its operation, and how it begins action, is utterly unknown to us: We are, however, without duly adverting to this, very apt to form conjectures concerning the requifites and manner of action, and even to convert thefe conjectures into fettled principles. And it is the more difficult to terminate difputes arifing upon this fubject, as the parties engaged in them are equally ignorant of the true nature of caufation.

THE great argument for abfolute neceffity, to the total exclufion of liberty, made ufe of by Mr Leibnitz and other ingenious writers who have adhered in general to his opinion, arifes from the following confideration: That a being fuppofed to be indued with active power, cannot begin to exert that power without

without some view or design, some motive or sufficient reason; and when such sufficient reason or motive occurs, the action must unavoidably follow. These things they affirm are so clear and evident, as that they cannot be controverted. And thus they make the beginning of action a necessary consequence of something prior to it, and would thereby take away the liberty of action altogether, and make it a link of a certain chain of events essentially connected together. And further, by having recourse to a preceeding reason, as the cause and motive of that which is immediately connected with the action, and so on without end, they are obliged to make the supposed chain infinite and eternal too.

We shall now endeavour shortly to examine and analyse this so much boasted argument.

THAT

That a being capable of beginning motion, or any action whatever, cannot do so without designing it, must certainly be allowed. This we have endeavoured to demonstrate formerly. And indeed, it is not conceivable how any action can begin by chance, and without any intention of the agent. And it may further be allowed, that there must be some motive or view of good which determines the agent to act or not, to do this or the contrary: For an agent may be indifferent as to a particular species of action; but may yet prefer action to rest. The great moment of the present controversy seems therefore to turn upon this point, Whether the motive previous to the action is necessarily connected with the action, and such as the agent cannot resist? or whether the motive is only of that nature as to influence

fluence the agent, but not necessarily, and so as to deprive him altogether of a power to resist it? Before we examine this point particularly, it may be observed, that the true resolution of it depends upon the perfect knowledge of the nature of causation, which, as we have not, we ought to be **modest and cautious** in all our reasonings and decisions in relation to it.

But let us try this matter by placing it in the several lights in which we are capable to perceive it. It will not surely be said to be a self-evident proposition, that the influence of a motive is necessary and irresistible, even when the agent gives way to it. Necessity is so strong and overbearing, according to our ideas of it, that it cannot admit of various degrees; for a less degree of necessity would be no necessity at all; whereas we are conscious

conscious that the influence of a motive admits of all possible degrees, some indeed so low, as hardly to be sensible at all. It is in consequence of this, that the mind is capable of deliberation; even when a motive is present, it does not immediately comply with its suggestion, but suspends action till it has duly examined its importance; and if it is satisfied of that, then it proceeds to exert its active power, in such a way, however, as to be conscious of liberty, and that it does not suffer any irresistible determination.

It may be questioned, whether any motive can be so strong as to produce an absolute necessity? But, without entering into any unnecessary dispute, it may be justly affirmed, that the motives upon which men commonly act, are of a far inferior nature, nay, often

so

so weak as hardly to be felt at all; to affirm then, that this influence is necessary, seems plainly to contradict the full and immediate conviction of the mind. When a man throws a stone out of his hand, its motion is necessary, and the stone cannot resist the power impelling it; but the action of the person who throws the stone appears in a very different light, and we discover nothing without the person as the cause of this action.

But it will be said, that there is a preceeding motive, in consequence of which the person performs the action. Be it so, yet it never can be shown or allowed that the consequence is necessary.

Let us examine the nature of a motive; it is surely not an active being, and cannot be an efficient cause; it is nothing but

but a quality, or mode of such a being; and it is the being itself that acts, which it could not be said to do if it was considered only as an instrument acted upon by one of its own modes. Be it allowed, that a motive is necessary in order to action; so also is thought; but neither of these is the proper cause of action: for they may both take place where there is no power to act at all. They can only be considered as requisites in an active being, in order to the exertion of its inherent power; a quality very different from these requisites, and in consequence of which alone it can act, as has already been observed.

Our imperfect knowledge of the nature of causation, seems to be the occasion of the perpetuated disputes in this matter. The view, however, above exhibited of the beginning of action, appears

pears to be the moſt ſimple, natural, and intelligible. It intirely appropriates the principle of action (than which nothing can appear more ſimple) to the nature of the active being itſelf: Whereas the contrary opinion moves every wheel of Nature and of Providence, and carries us through the interminable extent of immenſity and eternity, before any one ſingle action can take place: For it is to be obſerved, that thoſe who contend for the neceſſary influence of motives, when they are deſired to account for the motive immediately preceeding an action, they are obliged to have recourſe ſtill to an anterior motive, by means of which the laſt was produced; and they can ſtop at no privileged motive; but are forced to have recourſe to an infinite ſeries of events bound together in an endleſs chain: For, if we ſhould arrive at a motive which had no other motive

motive prior to it, then this motive muft have been produced without the affiftance of any preceeding one; which would be altogether inconfiftent with the hypothefis of the neceffitarians.

THESE philofophers, in reality, when they require a caufe of every thing; yet, by their manner of reafoning, oblige us to conclude, that there cannot be a caufe for any thing at all. In their fuppofed infinite chain of caufes and effects, or rather of different events neceffarily connected, we are led from one thing to another in order to arrive at the true and proper caufe of all; but at this we are not allowed to arrive, becaufe it would deftroy their argument; therefore, all the links of the chain are but mere neceffary effects, which yet neither have nor can have any real caufe at all. In reality, an infinite feries of different events,

vents, is a downright abfurdity and contradiction. Number and infinite are incompatible: Number is made up of units; but what is infinite cannot confift of finite parts, and excludes number altogether. This pretended demonftration of the neceffitarians is therefore a very unfortunate one. Before it can convince us, we muft underftand it; and in order to underftand it, we muft view it in its full extent. But then it takes fuch a boundlefs flight into immenfity and eternity, that we not only foon lofe fight of it, but turn fo giddy in the purfuit of it, that we are apt to lofe fight of every thing elfe.

But this intricate fubject is ftill perplexed by a diftinction which is made of neceffity, into what is called *moral* and *phyfical*. It is allowed, that phyfical neceffity is not applicable to an efficient caufe;

caufe; but at the fame time, it is contended, that moral neceffity muft be fo applied. It will be neceffary therefore to examine this diftinction with fome attention.

THOSE who contend for moral, in contradiftinction to phyfical neceffity, build their whole argument upon an erroneous notion they have formed with regard to the influence of motives. They alledge, that an intelligent and active being cannot begin action without fome view or motive exciting to act: And they further affirm, that the motive, in confequence of which action takes place, cannot be refifted; but that an intelligent and active being, under the influence of fuch motive, is determined by an abfolute neceffity to begin action. This laft propofition is certainly not felf-evident; and therefore muft
require

require a proof. It is not self-evident; for it is very easy to conceive, that an active being might have resisted the motive of action; and that therefore, when it gives way to it, it is not determined so to do by an absolute and fatal necessity. And it is so far from being capable of proof, that the contrary must appear evident from every view we are capable to take of the matter.

In reality, the distinction betwixt moral and physical necessity, upon which the necessitarians would found their reasoning, appears to be but a nominal, and not a real distinction: For, if moral necessity be as absolute and irresistible as physical necessity, it will be impossible to say in what sense an active being is not under physical necessity; or, in other words, is naturally free in the exertion of its power; and is yet, at the same time, under

der an absolute and irresistible moral necessity, which must totally deprive it of its freedom in every view we can take of that quality. It is vain therefore to hope for any advantage from a distinction which it is impossible to explain, or make common sense of.

But let us consider this matter in another view: If an intelligent and active being cannot exert the power of acting without being necessarily determined thereto, by the irresistible influence of some particular motive, this lands us in a palpable contradiction, as it totally confounds the ideas of action and passion: For that being which is necessarily and irresistibly determined in its operation, cannot with any propriety be said to act; it is at best but an instrument, and acted upon by another; and in the present case, by the motive whose
influence

influence is supposed to produce an absolute necessity. The motive therefore can only be considered as the proper efficient cause; and the being necessarily influenced by the motive can be considered as nothing else but an instrument by means of which the particular effect is produced. But it is evident that nothing can be more absurd than such a conclusion: For, to ascribe proper action, or the exertion of power, to the motive, and take it away from that being itself of which the motive is but an accidental mode or quality, is totally repugnant to our clearest ideas: For it is certainly most absurd to consider that being which still continues to exist, and to possess all the requisites of action, as a mere passive instrument, whilst we derive the true origin and exertion of power from what is but a transitory mode of such a being. If this argument

ment needed any illuftration, we might difcover its force in the cleareft manner, by applying it to the nature of that Being who is in himfelf the moft fimple, and the moft perfect, that is, the Deity.

THAT GOD always acts with defign, or from juft views and motives, muft certainly be admitted. It muft alfo be admitted, that the motives of action in the Deity are always conformable to the effential and **unchangeable perfections of his nature, and that** he cannot act otherways than as juftice and goodnefs fhall direct. He is not, however, upon this account, lefs free in his actions, becaufe he poffeffes within his own nature all the principles of action, and is abfolutely independent upon any other being. If we could fuppofe God to act capricioufly, fuch a capricious action furely would not indicate a greater degree

gree of liberty than a juſt and wiſe one; for liberty does not depend upon the nature of the action, but upon the manner of it, and the principle from which it flows.

THE power of God, as well as his other perfections, is indeed neceſſary and eternal; but the action or exertion of this power is temporary and tranſient; and it is here only where liberty can be diſcovered. Every being muſt indeed act according to its nature; and therefore there muſt be the greateſt conſtancy in the operations of the Deity, becauſe of all natures he is the moſt unchangeable. But ſurely, it would be abſurd to infer from this, that God had leſs liberty than any other being. His actions flow intirely from himſelf; he is the proper cauſe of them, as he poſſeſſes in himſelf all the principles of action in the

the moft independent manner: His actions indeed muft be juft and good, becaufe he is fo himfelf; but they muft alfo be free, becaufe it is God himfelf alone that acts in a manner the moft independent imaginable.

FROM the foregoing reflections, we may difcover the juftnefs of an obfervation which Seneca makes upon this fubject. He obferves, in his firft book of natural queftions, that God is always neceffarily pleafed with what is beft: And he adds, " Nec ob hoc minus li-
" ber ac potens eft; ipfe enim eft necef-
" fitas fua." God himfelf is the principle of this neceffity; and therefore it cannot in the leaft derogate from his power and liberty: For though he cannot do but what is beft; yet, as his actions only flow from his own nature and perfections, he is, in the moft perfect

AND NECESSITY.

fect fenfe of the word, the proper caufe and author of them; and confequently muft be free.

But, leaving thefe more abftrufe reafonings, let us now proceed to confider the matter in a more fimple and obvious point of light; let us fuppofe the cafe of two equipollent motives of action.

The neceffitarians, in explaining fuch a cafe, are greatly embarraffed: They are either obliged to fay, that no fuch cafe can exift; or, if it did, that an intelligent being could not act at all. With regard to the firft, to affert that two motives of action, in every refpect equal, cannot be prefented to the mind at the fame time, is an affirmation that has not the leaft reafon to fupport it. The idea of equality is as obvious, and as juft just as that of inequality, and wherever the one can be applied, so may the other; and though it should happen in fact, that no two things of the same kind are precisely equal; yet this would not in the least affect the general argument: For, admitting that no two bodies could be found in nature exactly equal; yet the reasonings of the mathematicians upon any supposed equality or inequality of bodies, would not be the less just and conclusive. The necessitarians are therefore forced to entrench themselves in the other member of the dilemma, and to maintain, That if two motives of action were entirely equal, the agent could not act at all. As no good reason can be given for so bold an assertion; so, if we give but the slightest attention to it, it must appear intirely false: For, let us suppose that there are two objects of happiness presented to the mind, intirely equal

equal with respect to every circumstance, and each of them easily to be attained, must the attainment of any one of them be impossible, because of that circumstance of equality? No surely; a general desire of happiness is a sufficient principle of action, which can never be disappointed, for that reason, that it may be easily gratified in two different ways.

Of this we must be intirely satisfied from the immediate consciousness we have of the active powers of the mind; nay, let us suppose several objects of action equally indifferent, and none of them of sufficient force to influence the mind, the very pleasure of action alone may have this effect; and when thus a sufficient motive of action exists, the mind will easily determine itself in the preference of any one of the supposed equal species or objects of action. And thus we clearly ly perceive how the mind acts, even when there is no prevailing motive to engage it; and we muſt alſo be ſatisfied, that it acts in the ſame manner, that is, freely, even when under the influence of ſuch motive.

The neceſſitarians ſometimes appeal to fact in proof of the truth of their doctrine, and alledge, that the conduct and actions of men are a neceſſary conſequence of their particular character and prevailing paſſions; and if the laſt are known, the firſt may be determined with great certainty. But this ſtill brings us back to the former queſtion, Whether the connection betwixt the conduct and paſſions of men is neceſſary, or only natural? That particular paſſions will influence a man's actions, is what none will deny; but then this influence is not neceſſary and irreſiſtible:

This

This muſt appear from the preceeding abſtract reaſonings, and is even confirmed from fact and obſervation: For, it muſt be allowed, that there are many inſtances of men who have ſubdued intirely the ſtrongeſt natural paſſions, by ſteadily purſuing a conduct contrary to what theſe would have led them to; and there is hardly any man who, upon ſome occaſions at leaſt, does not reſiſt his moſt favourite paſſion; ſo that, if experience proves a natural connection betwixt the character and the conduct, it proves at the ſame time, that that connection is not neceſſary; and though it may be the foundation of a very probable conjecture, yet it never can ſupport a certain concluſion.

It has already been obſerved, that the arguments urged by the neceſſitarians in favour of their peculiar doctrine,

X   are

are not pointed against any particular species of beings, but are drawn from the nature of the thing, and tend to persuade us, that liberty is in itself a thing impossible; and consequently, according to their opinion, the Supreme Being himself can have no liberty, but must be subjected to the fatal influence of the same absolute necessity. This consequence of itself might have sufficiently exposed the absurdity of the doctrine: For an **Almighty Being, possessing** in his own nature all the principles of action, and liable to no foreign influence whatever, must begin action in the most free and independent manner imaginable. Our ideas of the Deity seem to be no where clearer than in this matter; and though God will act always agreeably to his own perfections; yet still his acting is simple, absolute, and totally from himself, and his power is the

more

more perfect and divine, that it intirely agrees with his other attributes. But though freedom must certainly be allowed to belong to the Deity, it may still be a question, whether man is a free agent or not. However this may be determined, yet the greatest part of the difficulty is overcome, if we are satisfied that liberty is a possible thing; and in order to know whether it is applicable to men, it only remains to examine facts, and to consider the real qualities of human actions.

This indeed is not so much our present purpose; however, we may shortly observe, that from the consciousness we have of our own actions, we clearly distinguish them from the mere movements of a machine, in respect of which the machine is purely passive.

ALL

ALL the qualities of human actions correspond to the idea of liberty: Thus they are blameable or praise-worthy, morally good or evil, imputable, and consequently objects of reward and punishment: Hence man becomes a proper subject of moral government; and of the propriety of all these things we have a natural and immediate sense. Thus also our researches, deliberations, judgements, reasonings, and, in a word, the whole system of the human mind, has a manifest reference to liberty, without which it is not to be understood or accounted for.

LET us once for all reflect but a little upon what passes in the mind during the act of deliberating. Let us suppose, for instance, that finding ourselves uneasy under a state of indolence and inactivity, we resolve upon some exercise or other, but altogether in doubt what kind of exercise or action to prefer. In this case we carefully examine the several species of action which may occur, and compare them together; and we often continue this deliberation a considerable time before we make an election. It is supposed that the mind is resolved upon action, and would prefer the most indifferent one to a state of indolence and rest. The several species of action which we examine must therefore appear equal, otherways we could no longer deliberate, according to the opinion of the necessitarians, though, at the same time, they are not very willing to admit of such equality; but though they should be supposed equal when presented to the mind at the same time; yet, as they take place successively, the first in order of time, from that very circumstance, should prevail.

BUT

But it would be endless to pursue all the precarious suppositions which the necessitarians might make in order to render the mind a mere machine. The very consciousness of what passes in the mind whilst we deliberate affords a stronger evidence than a thousand arguments. We often resist motives when there is no real reason for so doing; and we are conscious, whilst we deliberate, that the mind holds the scales, and weighs and balances the force of the opposite motives, and then forms a final resolution with ease and with authority. It is not therefore a mere passive subject, the sport of contrary motives, which throw it into a giddy dance in an irresistible manner. No; we feel, whilst we deliberate, a secret power in the mind over the motives which may be presented to it, in virtue of which it suspends their influence; and when it yields to any
of

of them, it is still with this consciousness, that it could have resisted them; and that therefore the mind itself is properly the agent and by no means the motive.

It is indeed an inquiry too high for us to examine, in what manner, or to what degree, the power of acting is conferred upon us; we must be satisfied in general to know, that it is so from its unquestionable effects. It must, at the same time be allowed, that man, though a free, is yet a dependent and mixed being. He must depend upon his Supreme Creator for the exercise of his freedom; and also, in his sensations, desires, and affections, and in many other respects, he finds himself in a great measure passive. Such being the nature of the human mind, many difficult questions have been started in relation to the

the necessary concurrence of God, and the extent and degree of human liberty; and speculative men have often gone into opposite extremes, and that sometimes in a dogmatical manner: But, if we reflect on the imperfect condition of man, and the weakness of the human faculties, and are properly initiated in the principles of academical philosophy, we shall find reason to be modest and cautious in our decisions anent matters so abstruse and remote, and to rest satisfied with very general notions, instead of positive and particular opinions. Waving therefore such high debates, we shall proceed in our general examination of the nature of liberty, or the power of acting.

An ingenious writer (the author of the Essays of the Principles of Morality and Natural Religion), brings his argument

AND NECESSITY.

ment in support of necessity within the following narrow compass: "The pre-
"ceeding reasoning," says he, " may
" perhaps make a stronger impression by
" being reduced to a short argument, af-
" ter this manner. No man can be con-
" ceived to act without some principle
" leading him to action. All our prin-
" ciples of action resolve into desires
" and aversions; for nothing can prompt
" us to move or exert ourselves in any
" shape but what presents some object
" to be pursued or avoided. A motive
" is an object so operating upon the
" mind as to produce either desire or a-
" version. Now, liberty, as opposite to
" moral necessity, must signify a power
" in the mind of acting without or a-
" gainst motives; that is to say, a power
" of acting without any view, pur-
" pose, or design, and even acting in
" contradiction to our own desires
" and aversions; which power, be-
" sides

"sides that no man was ever consci-
"ous of it, seems to be an absurdity al-
"together inconsistent with a rational
"nature."

We shall not enter into a particular analysis of this pretended demonstration, but only make a few general remarks upon it in consequence of our preceeding reasoning. It is not true, that we always act in consequence of a motive; for we may act when motives are equal. This our author candidly admits; he adds indeed, that this case must be extremely rare, and therefore not much to be regarded. But the importance of the observation consists in this, that when in any one plain instance we clearly discover liberty, we justly infer, that it is a natural quality of the agent; and therefore that it is to be ascribed to it in other cases that may appear more ambiguous: For, another observation to be be made is, that when the mind acts from motives, it does not act necessarily, but has a power to resist these motives. This is the great point upon which the present dispute turns; and it appears to be sufficiently illustrated from the preceeding observation; for if, in any instance, the mind can act without propellent motives, we may naturally suppose, that even when such motives take place, its action may resist them; nay, if it was otherways, and that the motive, by an absolute necessity, produced the action of the mind, it would be the greatest impropriety to say, that the mind acted at all: For in this case it must be intirely passive, and can only be considered as an instrument acted upon, and we must search for the proper and efficient cause of the action, either in the motive itself, or we must ascend higher to something preceeding the motive,

motive, till at laſt we arrive at the true ſource and origin of the action, where liberty muſt certainly take place; unleſs we ſhall adopt the abſurd and contradictory notion of an infinite ſeries.

THE preceeding reaſoning muſt ſufficiently demonſtrate, that when the mind acts from motives, it is not determined by an abſolute neceſſity; whereas the contrary opinion not only involves us in the groſſeſt abſurdities, but is a mere aſſertion without any evidence to ſupport it: For, when an action flows from a motive, we are by no means obliged to admit, that it flows neceſſarily from it. The natural effect of an action is indeed neceſſary; but the proper cauſe of it muſt be free, otherways it cannot with propriety be ſaid to act, but muſt be conſidered as a mere paſſive inſtrument. We ſhall only obſerve further, with regard to to the reasoning of the author we have mentioned, that he considers liberty as a power of acting without any view or design; but this is an improper representation of the matter: For the question is not properly, whether the mind acts with any design or motive, which must be allowed, at least, to be commonly the case? but whether that design or motive necessarily determines the mind to act? Which must be denied, otherways the mind could not be said to act at all: And whereas he says, to act without a motive, is inconsistent with a rational nature; this is losing sight of the true state of the question, which is not so much, whether the mind can act without a motive? as whether such motive necessarily determines the mind? And, if this last should be said, it would seem indeed to be inconsistent with a rational nature: For the motive determining

mining the mind, by an abfolute neceffity, to action, (if this term can with a-
ny propriety be ufed), muft prevent the
calm and fpeculative principle of reafon
from reflecting upon the nature of the
action, and the genuine confequences of
it.

It feems unneceffary to purfue this
abftrufe fubject any further; for, if any
doubt fhould ftill remain with regard to
the reality of liberty, this muft be intirely owing to the imperfection of our
ideas in relation to the firft exertion of
power; an imperfection which will e-
ver remain, fo long as our faculties continue in their prefent ftate. However,
if we leave thefe metaphyfical and fubtile fpeculations, and form our opinions upon the common occurrences of
life, and thofe ideas which are moft obvious and familiar, we can never hefi-
tate

tate a moment in determining whether we are free agents, or mere paffive machines. The idea of liberty entirely tallies with every thing that falls under our experience, and its propriety is confpicuous in relation to the univerfal government of God, and alfo to every fpecies of human government.

It muft not, however, be diffembled, that there are objections brought againft liberty too material to be overlooked; and yet drawn from fuch remote and hidden fources, as that they are to be examined with great modefty and caution: Thefe fources are the Divine Prefcience, and Divine Decrees.

It is alledged, that liberty is altogether inconfiftent with the Divine prefcience; and indeed this opinion has appeared in fo ftrong a light, that it has forced

forced philosophers and divines into opposite extremes, whilst some chose to take away liberty, and others to overthrow the Divine prescience; yet these perhaps may be reconciled, and the difficulty may arise not from the real inconsistency betwixt the things themselves, but from the great imperfection of our ideas.

WHAT may be the true foundation of the Divine prescience, we cannot pretend to tell. Setting revelation aside, we have indeed no other means of knowing future events, but from the connection of cause and effect, and that necessary order of things which is thereby established. But it would surely be the highest presumption in us to circumscribe the Divine knowledge by the scanty model of our very weak faculties. It may be observed with regard
to

to all actions and events whatever, which really take place, that it may be affirmed of them from all eternity that they would exist. And this is true not only with regard to those events which are the necessary effects of irresistible causes, but also of the beginning of action itself, or of the first and free exertion of active power, independent of any preceeding cause: And thus there is a difference betwixt certainty and necessity, founded in the nature of things. Necessity is a quality that can only be applied to an event which exists in consequence of the irresistible influence of a proper cause; but certainty is applicable not only to such event, but also to the action of the cause itself, however free that may be supposed to be. This distinction is taken notice of by Cicero in his book *De Fato*, in the following words: " Licet enim Epicuro, con-

" cedenti

" cedenti omne enunciatum aut verum,
" aut falsum esse, non vereri, ne omnia
" fato fieri sit necesse: non enim æternis
" causis naturæ necessitate manantibus
" verum est id, quod ita enuntiatur.
" Descendit in Academiam Carneades:
" nec tamen sine causis: sed interest in-
" ter causas fortuito antegressas, et in-
" ter causas cohibentes in se efficientiam
" naturalem."

Now, though the necessity arising from a series of causes and effects, is alone what can enable us to look into futurity; yet the certainty, even from all eternity, of the existence of an event, though the immediate effect of liberty, and no part of a necessary concatenation of things, may be a sufficient foundation for the Divine prescience. It is true, we cannot form any particular idea of this matter; but we ought to remember,
that

that the Divine knowledge is infinitely superior to ours, both in kind and degree; besides, the other perfections of God are as inscrutable to us.

Can we explain God's eternal existence, which seems to unite past, present, and to come, and thereby to render future events the objects of his knowledge, as well as those that are past? Can we conceive creative power, or how a thing is brought to existence from nothing? Yet these perfections we must necessarily allow to the Deity, however imperfect our ideas of them may be. We need not then be surprised if the Divine knowledge is too great an object for our capacity, which is infinitely disproportioned to the Divine perfections.

We must be contented to have pointed out certainty as the foundation of the Divine

Divine knowledge in relation to future events of whatever kind. And though we are not able to connect thefe; yet this is at leaft taking one ftep, which we are not even able to do with regard to creative power. Indeed, if the imperfection of our ideas is a juft objection to the Divine prefcience, we muft, for the fame reafon, take away all the other perfections of God at once.

But let us further proceed to confider the Decrees of God; and in this refpect the difficulty will appear to be greatly increafed. As all things have proceeded from God, nothing appears more reafonable than to confider them as intirely fubjected to his fovereign will and power; yet this opinion feems abfolutely to exclude liberty, not only as it creates a difficulty in reconciling it with the Divine decrees, but as it

places

places the one in a direct oppofition to the other. This difficulty may, however, be refolvable into the weaknefs and imperfection of our minds. The Divine prefcience may be a foundation for the Divine decrees, which muft be viewed in a very different light as they relate to free agents, and as they relate to beings intirely paffive and inert; and though we cannot pretend to fee this difference in a true and proper light; yet this is nothing uncommon in matters fo arduous and fublime.

The contemplation of the immenfity, eternity, and the other perfections of God, rather confounds and aftonifhes than enlightens our minds. And that is often trueft which we are ready to pronounce impoffible. It becomes us, therefore, to be modeft, and to fuppofe there

there may be a method of explaining the Divine decrees fo as to reconcile them with liberty, our ignorance of which ought not at all to furprife us.

Mankind, from the earlieft ages, according to their loofe and general notions, (and thefe are all we can have in this matter,) allowed both of decrees and liberty. Thus Homer, who wrote according the prevailing opinions, in the beginning of the firft book of the Iliad, affirms, that all things (having in his view even the free actions of men) were accomplifhed by the will of Jupiter.

> Such was the fovereign will, and fuch the doom of Jove.

The fame great poet as ftrenuoufly afferts liberty by the authority of Jupiter himfelf; towards the beginning of the Odyffey,

Odyssey, he introduces Jupiter speaking in the following manner.

> Perverse mankind, whose will's created free,
> Charge all their woes on absolute decree;
> All to the dooming gods their guilt translate,
> And follies are miscall'd the crimes of fate.

BUT, whatever opinion we may form to ourselves of the Divine decrees, we are not to imagine that these can lay any improper restraint upon the Divine conduct, or obstruct what is fittest and best to be done in any circumstances; for this would be making the decrees of God superior to God himself, and repugnant to his moral character and perfections. As therefore the government of God is moral, we need not be afraid that the decrees of God will, in any case, obstruct any fit or proper moral effect. Indeed, in matters so sublime and abstruse, modesty is our truest wisdom;

wifdom; and it is fafer to confefs our ignorance, than rafhly to embrace any particular opinion, which can hardly fail to be erroneous: Ignorance in fuch a cafe is more excufcable than error, which is generally accompanied with fome degree of prefumption.

Instead, therefore, of purfuing a fubject fo very difficult and abftrufe, it may be of much greater ufe and benefit to us, to confider the natural tendency and confequences of the different opinions of liberty and neceffity.

If we fhall think that we are free, and that we have within ourfelves the proper principles of action, we muft at the fame time be fenfible, that our happinefs depends in a great meafure upon ourfelves; for happinefs or mifery muft, by the invariable order of nature, be the
fruit

fruit of our own doings: If we shall then have this persuasion, that we have a real power over our own conduct, such persuasion will engage us in the most effectual manner to prefer such conduct as leads to happiness; and consequently we will exert every power of the soul in the constant pursuit of virtue, than which nothing can more effectually promote the happiness of others, as well as that of ourselves.

But, on the other hand, if we shall embrace the opinion of necessity, then we must consider ourselves as mere machines only, acted upon, but without any power of action. Such opinion must relax all the vigour of the soul, must damp and discourage every generous emotion of the mind, and indeed, tend to reduce us to a state of total indifference and stupidity; than which nothing can be more pernicious to society as well as to the individual.

These very different consequences of the opposite doctrines of liberty and necessity, may have no small weight in determining upon what side the truth lies; for, as liberty entirely tallies with the whole system of the human mind, particularly with the most important quality of virtue; it is therefore ~~naturally applicable~~ to man; whereas, necessity being the reverse of all this, is inconsistent with all our ideas of a rational and active being, and can only be applied to a mere passive machine. And these are the conclusions which we naturally make, when we are freed from the influence of certain abstruse speculations which we are

not

not able to comprehend, and which totally confound the distinction betwixt action and passion, betwixt the voluntary operations of an intelligent agent, and the necessary movements of a mere machine; a distinction universally allowed by the common sense of mankind.

THE END.

ERRATA.

P. 89. l. 12. For *virtues*, read *vortices*.
P. 105. l. antepen. For *single*, read *simple*.
P. 113. l. antepen. For *compound*, read *component*.
P. 119. l. 9. For *compound*, read *component*.

www.ingramcontent.com/pod-product-compliance
Lightning Source LLC
Chambersburg PA
CBHW020848160426
43192CB00007B/828